ROYAL COURT

Royal Court Theatre presents

PLASTICINE

by **Vassily Sigarev**
translated by Sasha Dugdale

First performance at the Royal Court Jerwood Theatre Upstairs
Sloane Square, London on 15 March 2002.

The International Playwrights Season is presented in association with the Genesis Foundation and
developed in collaboration with the British Council.

•••••• The
•••••• British
•••••• Cour

ROYAL COURT

INTERNATIONAL PLAYWRIGHTS SEASON 2002

in association with the Genesis Foundation

8 February - 2 March

push up by Roland Schimmelpfennig

Translated by Maja Zade
Directed by Ramin Gray

6 - 9 March

Theatre Lozhe, Kemerovo and Babii, Chelyabinsk

steps to siberia

Visiting companies from the Urals and Siberia

15 March – 6 April

plasticine by Vassily Sigarev

Translated by Sasha Dugdale
Directed by Dominic Cooke

28 February - 6 April

human rights focus

Events and readings of specially commissioned plays responding to the most pressing issues of the moment from: **Argentina, Belgium, Brazil, Colombia, France, Germany, Italy, Palestine, Romania, Russia, Spain, UK, USA**
including:

I March **FOCUS: Palestine**
9 and 13 March **FOCUS: Russia**
25 March **FOCUS: Immigration and Asylum**
26 March **FOCUS: South America**

The International Playwrights Season is developed in collaboration with the British Council

For full details please contact the box office on: 020 7565 5000

PLASTICINE

by **Vassily Sigarev**
translated by Sasha Dugdale

Cast
Man in Window/Sedoy **Daniel Cerqueira**
Lyokha **Bryan Dick**
Cadet/Groom **Matthew Dunster**
Ludmila/2nd Old Woman/Woman Having Sex **Molly Innes**
1st Woman/Lyokha's Mother **Liz Kettle**
Maksim **Michael Legge**
Grandmother/2nd Woman **Mary Macleod**
Headmaster/Neighbour **John Rogan**
Spira/Boy Having Sex **Russell Tovey**
Tanya/Bride **Myfanwy Waring**
Natasha/Tanya's Mother **Liz White**
All other roles played by members of the company

Director **Dominic Cooke**
Designer **Ian MacNeil**
Costume Designer **Joan Wadge**
Lighting Designer **Johanna Town**
Sound Designer **Paul Arditti**
Movement Director **Liz Ranken**
Composer **Gary Yershon**
Assistant Director **Neran Persaud**
Casting Director **Lisa Makin**
Production Manager **Sue Bird**
Company Stage Manager **Cath Binks**
Stage Management **Suzanne Bourke, Emily Danby**
Student Stage Manager **Jo Brown**
Costume Supervisor **Iona Kenrick**
Student Costume Designer **Sibylla Parkhill**
Dialect Coach **Penny Dyer**
Fight Director **Terry King**
Company Voice Work **Patsy Rodenburg**

Royal Court Theatre would like to thank the following for their help with this production:
Wardrobe care by Persil and Comfort courtesy of Lever Fabergé.

THE COMPANY

Vassily Sigarev (writer)
For the Royal Court: Plasticine (rehearsed reading New Plays From Russia, 2001), Black Milk (rehearsed reading, International Playwrights Season 2002).
Other plays includes: The Vampire's Family, The Lie Detector, The Russian Lottery, Black Milk.
Awards include: Anti-Booker Prize (Plasticine 2000), Debut Prize (Plasticine 2000), Eureka Prize (Black Milk 2002).

Paul Arditti (sound designer)
Paul Arditti has been designing sound for theatre since 1983. He currently combines his post as Head of Sound at the Royal Court (where he has designed more than 60 productions) with regular freelance projects.
Royal Court productions include: Boy Gets Girl, Nightingale and Chase, Sliding With Suzanne (co-production with Out of Joint), Clubland, Blasted, Mouth To Mouth, Spinning Into Butter, I Just Stopped By To See The Man, Far Away, My Zinc Bed, 4.48 Psychosis, Fireface, Mr Kolpert, The Force of Change, Hard Fruit, Other People, Dublin Carol, The Glory of Living, The Kitchen, Rat in the Skull, Some Voices, Mojo, The Weir; The Steward of Christendom, Shopping and Fucking, Blue Heart (co-productions with Out of Joint); The Chairs (co-production with Theatre de Complicite); Cleansed, Via Dolorosa.
Other theatre includes: Hinterland (Out of Joint); Afore Night Come (Young Vic); Tales From Hollywood (Donmar); Light (Complicite); Our Lady of Sligo (RNT with Out of Joint); Some Explicit Polaroids (Out of Joint); Hamlet, The Tempest (RSC); Orpheus Descending, Cyrano de Bergerac, St Joan (West End); Marathon (Gate).
Musicals include: Doctor Dolittle, Piaf, The Threepenny Opera.
Awards include: Drama Desk Award for Outstanding Sound Design 1992 for Four Baboons Adoring the Sun (Broadway).

Daniel Cerqueira
For the Royal Court: Mountain Language/ Ashes To Ashes, Cleansed, Attempts on Her Life, The Crutch (Young Writers Festival 1998), Bintou (International Playwrights Season 2000).
Other theatre includes: Afore Night Come (Young Vic); Two Tigers (Edinburgh Festival); Caledonian Road (White Bear); Blue Vienna (Hampstead); Ten Years of Freedom, Crocodile Looking at Birds (Lyric, Hammersmith); Courting Winona (Old Red Lion); Waking Beauty (Arts Threshold); Days of Hope (Oxford Stage Co.); The Brave (Bush); Handsome, Handicapped and Hebrew (Grove); Antony and Cleopatra (Moving Theatre Company); The Art of Random Whistling, The People Downstairs (Young Vic); Aunt Dan and Lemon (Almeida); Powder Keg (Gate); Meat (Plymouth Theatre Royal); Luminosity (RSC); While Waiting at My Mother's Vigil (BAC).
Television includes: Pirate Prince, Hot Dog Wars, City Central, Sunburn.
Film includes: Fuel, Valley Girls, Saving Private Ryan, Toy Boys, Mad Cows, Tube Tales.

Dominic Cooke (director)
Associate Director of the Royal Court.
For the Royal Court: Fucking Games, Redundant, Spinning into Butter, Fireface, Other People.
Other theatre includes: As adapter and director: Arabian Nights (Young Vic/UK and world tour/ New Victory Theatre, New York); The Marriage of Figaro (tour). As director: Hunting Scenes From Lower Bavaria, The Weavers (Gate), Afore Night Come, Entertaining Mr Sloane (Theatr Clwyd); The Bullet (Donmar Warehouse); My Mother Said I Never Should (Oxford Stage Company/ Young Vic); Of Mice and Men (Nottingham Playhouse); Kiss Of the Spiderwoman (Bolton Octagon); Autogeddon (Edinburgh Assembly Rooms); Caravan (National Theatre of Norway); The Importance of Being Earnest (Atlantic Theatre Festival, Canada).
Opera includes: I Capuleti e i Montacchi (Grange Park Opera).
Awards include: TMA Award for Arabian Nights, Manchester Evening News Drama Award for The Marriage of Figaro and Edinburgh Fringe First for Autogeddon.
Assistant Director at the Royal Shakespeare Company 1992-94.

Bryan Dick
For the Royal Court: Sliding with Suzanne (co-production with Out of Joint).
Other theatre includes: School Play (Soho Theatre).
Television includes: Mersey Beat, Dalziel and Pascoe, Strange, The Bill, Dance with an Angel, Clocking Off 2, Losing It, North Square, Shockers II, The Life and Times of Henry Pratt, Bonjour La Class, Earthfasts, Speaking in Tongues.
Film includes: Morvern Caller, Dream.

Sasha Dugdale (translator)
Sasha has translated several Russian plays for the Royal Court, including How I Ate a Dog by Evgeny Grishkovets, U by Olga Mukhina and Vassily Sigarev's most recent play Black Milk.

Matthew Dunster
For the Royal Court: Toast.
Other theatre includes: The Outsider, The Trial, The Mill On The Floss (Contact Theatre); But the Living are Wrong in The Sharp Distinctions They Make, Nest of Spices, The Wasp Factory, (Northern Stage); Happy Families (Derby Playhouse); Road (Royal Exchange); Fallen Angels (Fecund Theatre); Flying (RNT Studio).
Television includes: Heartbeat, Coronation Street, Gimme, Gimme, Gimme, A Great Deliverance, Casualty, Always & Everyone, Spring Hill, Brookside, Two Minutes, Golden Collar, Into the Fire, Walking on the Moon.
Film includes: Peaches.
Writing includes: You Used To (Contact Theatre); Tell Me (Contact, Northern Stage, Donmar Warehouse); The Glazier (British Council Tour); To You (the inaugural dramatic poem for the Lowry Centre, Salford); Two Clouds Over Eden (Royal Exchange Theatre); Depth of Field (BBC Radio Four).

Molly Innes
Theatre includes: Electra (Theatre Babel, Ian Charleson Award Commendation); Moving Objects (Brunton Theatre, Stage Nomination Best Actress); A Listening Heaven (Lyceum); Antigone (TAG Theatre); A Solemn Mass for a Full Moon In Summer, Widows, Shining Souls, Stones and Ashes, Cross Dressing in the Depression (Traverse); Timeless (Suspect Culture); Jekyll and Hyde, To Kill a Mockingbird, The Prime of Miss Jean Brodie (Royal Lyceum); Doing Bird (Cat 'A' Theatre and UK tour); Playboy of the Western World (Theatre Communicado, Edinburgh); The Stinging Sea (Citizens Theatre); Tartuffe (Dundee Repertory Theatre).
Television includes: Rebus, The Bill, A Mug's Game, Strathblair, Rab C Nesbitt, Taking Over the Asylum, The Ferguson Theory, Trev and Simon.
Film includes: Karmic Mothers, Ratcatcher.
Radio includes: The Fourth Foreigner, Bill 'n' Koo, Some of My Best Friends are Dolphins.

Liz Kettle
For the Royal Court: The Desire Paths, A Girl Skipping.
Other theatre includes: Iphigenia (Abbey, Dublin); Spin (White Bear & Battersea Arts Centre); Digging for Ladies (tour); Body of a Woman (Brighton Festival); The Tempest (Union of European Theatres); The Storm, After the Fire (Gate); Henry VI: The Battle for The Throne (RSC, national & international tour); The House of Bernarda Alba (Gate); The Clink (Paines Plough); War Dance (Lumiere & Son); The Journeywoman (Mercury Theatre, Colchester); Alice in Wonderland (Theatre de Complicite).
Television includes: Alistair McGowan's Big Impressions, Hawkins, The Bill, Poirot, A Wing & A Prayer, Real Women, Staying Alive, Drop the Dead Donkey, Barry Welsh is Coming, Paris, The Vision Thing, The Story of Philip Knight, Lovejoy, Calling the Shots, Fatal Inversion, Nicholas Craig Masterclass, Jeeves and Wooster, Inspector Morse, Ruth Rendell's: A Sleeping Life, Capital City, Arm in Arm Together.
Radio includes: Daughters of Britannia.

Michael Legge
For the Royal Court: Presence.
Other theatre includes: Cressida (Albery).
Television includes: The Precious Blood.
Film includes: Whatever Happened to Harold Smith, Angela's Ashes, Stray Dogs, Soft Sand Blue Sea.
Radio includes: Othello, A Thousand Ships.
Michael was nominated Best Newcomer by the London Film Critics' Circle for Angela's Ashes.

Mary Macleod

For the Royal Court: Blue Heart (co-production
Out of Joint), Hammet's Apprentice, All Things
Nice, The Farm, One at Night, Life Price, Macbeth,
Three Men for Colverton, Minatures .
Other theatre includes: The Long Way Round,
Racing Demon, When We Were Women,
Entertaining Strangers, Neaptide, The Garden of
England, Inner Voices, Much Ado About Nothing,
The Prince of Homburg, Serjeant Musgrave's
Dance, A Month in the Country, Equus (RNT);
Hunting for Dragons, Belle Fontaine (Soho);
Orpheus Descending (Theatre Royal, Haymarket);
Scrape Off The Black, Black Man's Burden
(Riverside Studios); Butterfly Kiss (Almeida); The
Soldier's Song (Theatre Royal, Stratford East);
Henry IV, Parts I & II (English Touring Company/Old
Vic); Easter, The Widowing of Mrs Holroyd
(Leicester Haymarket); The Marriage of Figaro
(Palace Theatre, Watford); Vieux Carré
(Nottingham Playhouse).
Television includes: Prescription for Murder,
Brotherly Love, The Bill, Madame Bovary, The
Witches of Pendle, The Aerodrome, Farmer's
Arms, The Rector's Wife, The Best of British, John
Daniel, Brideshead Revisited, Mapp and Lucia, The
Singing Detective, Taggart, Taking Over the Asylum,
A Mug's Game, Dalziel and Pascoe.
Films include: Enigma, The House of Mirth, I Want
You, Restoration, Venus Peter, Hear My Song,
Orlando, Brimstone, Britannia Hospital, O Lucky
Man, 'If...".

Ian MacNeil (designer)

For the Royal Court: Far Away, Via Dolorosa (and
Broadway), This is a Chair, Body Talk, The Editing
Process, Death and the Maiden (also national tour).
Other theatre includes: Afore Night Come (Young
Vic); Albert Speer, Machinal (RNT); An Inspector
Calls (RNT, West End, Broadway, international);
The Ingolstadt Plays, Figaro Gets Divorced, Jerker
(Gate); Enter Achilles, Bound to Please (DV8).
Opera includes: Medea (Opera North); Tristan and
Isolde, Der Freischutz (ENO); Ariodante (ENO and
Welsh Opera); La Traviata (Paris, Opera); Il Ritorno
d'Ulisse in Patria (Munich Opera).
Film and television includes: Winterriese (Channel
4), Eight (Working Title), The Hours (Paramount,
Associate Producer).
In 1999 Ian designed costumes and environments
for the Pet Shop Boys album Nightlife and staged
the world tour following its release.

Neran Persaud (assistant director)

As director, theatre includes: Papa Was a Bus
Conductor (Edinburgh Festival/Lyric Studio
Theatre/Leicester Haymarket/Green Room,
Manchester); Made in England (Green Room,
Manchester); Don't Look at my Sister
(Edinburgh Festival/Bloomsbury/Warwick Arts
Centre/national tour); Bollywood or Bust
(national tour); Arrange That Marriage
(Bloomsbury/Leicester Haymarket/
Watermans Art Centre).

John Rogan

Theatre includes: The Playboy of the Western
World, Peer Gynt, The Cripple of Inishmaan,
The Machine Wreckers (RNT); Richard II
(RNT/Salzburg/Paris); Volpone, Don Carlos,
The School for Scandal (RSC Stratford/
Barbican); The Iceman Cometh (Almeida/Old
Vic); The Loves of Cass McGuire (Druid
Theatre Company); Loot, Entertaining Mr
Sloane (Birmingham Rep); On Borrowed
Time (Southwark Playhouse); The
Matchmaker, Love's Labours Lost, Culture
Vulture, Victory, The Rivals, Reunion in
Vienna (Chichester Festival); Cat's Play, Born
Yesterday (Greenwich); La Bete, Public
Enemy (Lyric, Hammersmith); Our Town
(Shaftesbury); The Plough and the Stars
(Young Vic); Into the Woods (Phoenix
Theatre); London Assurance (Haymarket);
Observe the Sons of Ulster Marching
Towards the Somme (Hampstead); The
Saxon Shore (Almeida); Love's Labour' Lost,
Richard III, Dreamplay, Henry V, All's Well
That Ends Well, Henry IV, A Winter's Tale, A
Midsummer Night's Dream (RSC Stratford &
Barbican); All's Well That Ends Well (Martin
Beck Theatre, New York); Juno & The
Paycock (Olivier Award Nomination, RSC
Aldwych); Much Ado About Nothing, The
Caucasian Chalk Circle, The Loud Boy's Life
(RSC tour); Happy End (Oxford Playhouse
Company).
Television includes: Weirdsister College,
Father Ted, The Bill, Broken Glass,
Woodcock, The Buddha Of Suburbia, Making
Out, Poirot, Boon, The Case of the Late Pig,
Small World, Porterhouse Blue, Squaring the
Circle, Dangerous Davies.
Film includes: Doctor Sleep, Richard II,
Drowning by Numbers, The Old Jest, Foreign
Body, Caravaggio, Scum.
Radio includes: RTE radio programmes, My
Sky Blue Trades, Crime and Punishment, Still
Time, Raising Patrick Doherty, Silver's City,
Best Words.

Russell Tovey
Theatre includes: Howard Katz (RNT); The Recruiting Officer (Chichester); Troy (Minerva). Television includes: Ultimate Force, NCS, Poirot: Evil Under the Sun, Holby City, The Bill, Suffocation, Hope & Glory, Anchor Me, Lily & The Learning Seed, Mud, Mrs Bradley Mysteries, Sort It, Spywatch.
Film: The Emperor's New Clothes, The Red Peppers.

Johanna Town (lighting designer)
Johanna has been Head of Lighting for the Royal Court since 1990 and has designed extensively for the company during this time.
Productions include: Fucking Games, Nightingale and Chase, Sliding With Suzanne (co-production with Out of Joint), I Just Stopped By To See The Man, Under the Blue Sky, Mr Kolpert, Other People, Toast, The Kitchen, Faith Healer, Pale Horse, Search and Destroy. Other recent theatre designs include: Hinterland (Out of Joint/RNT); Top Girls (Aldwych/West End/OSC); Les Liaison Dangereuses (Liverpool Playhouse); Feelgood (Out of Joint/ Hampstead/ Garrick); Playboy of the Western World (Liverpool Playhouse); Rita, Sue and Bob Too, A State Affair (Out of Joint/Soho Theatre); Arabian Nights (New Victory, New York); Ghosts (Royal Exchange Theatre); Our Lady of Sligo (Irish Repertory Theatre, New York); Rose (RNT/ Broadway); Little Malcolm (Hampstead/ West End); Our Country's Good (Young Vic/Out of Joint); Blue Heart (Royal Court/Out of Joint/ New York); Tobias and the Angel (Almeida Opera Festival).

Gary Yershon (composer)
For the Royal Court: Redundant, Fireface, Hysteria, Inventing a New Colour.
Other theatre includes: The Play What I Wrote (Wyndhams), Boston Marriage (Donmar/New Ambassadors); The Magic Toyshop, A Doll's House (Shared Experience); Twelfth Night, The Rivals, The Taming of the Shrew, Don Carlos, Hamlet, The Unexpected Man, As You Like It, The Merchant of Venice, Artists and Admirers, The Virtuoso (RSC); Tartuffe, Life x 3, Further Than the Furthest Thing, Widowers' Houses, Troilus and Cressida, The Way of the World, The Tempest, Broken Glass, Pericles (RNT); Marathon, Hunting Scenes from Lower Bavaria, The Weavers (Gate); Arabian Nights, Miss Julie (Young Vic); Peter Pan, The Government Inspector, A Perfect Ganesh, Death of a Salesman, The Hypochondriac, Don Juan (West Yorkshire Playhouse); Art (London/New York/Worldwide); Doña Rosita the Spinster (Almeida).
Television includes: Painted Tales, James the Cat. Film includes: Topsy-Turvy.
Radio includes: Ruslan and Lyudmila, The Wasting Game, In the Solitude of the Cotton Fields, Room of Leaves.

Myfanwy Waring
Theatre includes: Under Milk Wood (Theatr Clwyd).
Film includes: Unrequited, Daylight Robbery.

Liz White
Theatre includes: The Woman Who Walked into Doors (Stephen Joseph Theatre); A Midsummer Night's Dream (Wales Actors Co). Film & television includes: Ultimate Force, A&E, Auf Wiedersehen Pet, Hidden City, A Good Thief, Close Up North, Faced, Antidote Wanted, Anybody Out There.

REBUILDING THE ROYAL COURT

In 1995, the Royal Court was awarded a National Lottery grant through the Arts Council of England, to pay for three quarters of a £26m project to completely rebuild its 100-year old home. The rules of the award required the Royal Court to raise £7.6m in partnership funding. The building has been completed thanks to the generous support of those listed below.

We are particularly grateful for the contributions of over 5,700 audience members.

English Stage Company Registered Charity number 231242.

THE AMERICAN FRIENDS OF THE ROYAL COURT THEATRE

AFRCT support the mission of the Royal Court and are primarily focused on raising funds to enable the theatre to produce new work by emerging American writers. Since this not-for-profit organisation was founded in 1997, AFRCT has contributed to seven productions including Rebecca Gilman's Boy Gets Girl. They have also supported the participation of young artists in the Royal Court's acclaimed International Residency.

If you would like to support the ongoing work of the Royal Court, please contact the Development Department on 020 7565 5050.

THE ARTS COUNCIL OF ENGLAND

PROGRAMME SUPPORTERS

The Royal Court (English Stage Company Ltd) receives its principal funding from London Arts. It is also supported financially by a wide range of private companies and public bodies and earns the remainder of its income from the box office and its own trading activities.
The Royal Borough of Kensington & Chelsea gives an annual grant to the Royal Court Young Writers' Programme and the London Boroughs Grants Committee provides project funding for a number of play development initiatives.

The Jerwood Charitable Foundation continues to support new plays by new playwrights through the Jerwood New Playwrights series. Since 1993 the A.S.K. Theater Projects of Los Angeles has funded a Playwrights' Programme at the theatre. Bloomberg Mondays, the Royal Court's reduced price ticket scheme, is supported by Bloomberg.

TRUSTS AND FOUNDATIONS
American Friends of the Royal Court Theatre
Anon
The Carnegie United Kingdom Trust
Carlton Television Trust
Gerald Chapman Fund
The Foundation for Sport and the Arts
Genesis Foundation
The Goldsmiths' Company
Jerwood Charitable Foundation
John Lyon's Charity
The Laura Pels Foundation
Quercus Charitable Trust
The Peggy Ramsay Foundation
The Peter Jay Sharp Foundation
The Royal Victoria Hall Foundation
The Sobell Foundation
The Trusthouse Charitable Foundation
Garfield Weston Foundation

MAJOR SPONSORS
Amerada Hess
A.S.K. Theater Projects
AT&T: *OnStage*
BBC
Bloomberg
Channel Four
Royal College of Psychiatrists

BUSINESS MEMBERS
BP
CGNU plc
J Walter Thompson
Lazard
Lever Fabergé
McCABES
Pemberton Greenish
Peter Jones
Redwood
SIEMENS
Simons Muirhead & Burton

INDIVIDUAL MEMBERS
Patrons
Anon
Advanpress
Mark Bentley
Katie Bradford

Mrs Alan Campbell-Johnson
David Coppard
Chris Corbin
David Day
Mrs Phillip Donald
Thomas Fenton
Ralph A Fields
John Flower
Edna & Peter Goldstein
Homevale Ltd
Tamara Ingram
Mr & Mrs Jack Keenan
Barbara Minto
New Penny Productions Ltd
Martin Newson
AT Poeton & Son Ltd.
André Ptaszynski, Really Useful Theatres
Caroline Quentin
William & Hilary Russell
Ian & Carol Sellars
Miriam Stoppard
Carl & Martha Tack
Jan & Michael Topham
Mr & Mrs Anthony Weldon
Richard Wilson OBE
Amanda Vail

Benefactors
Anon
Anastasia Alexander
Lesley E Alexander
Mr & Mrs J Attard-Manché
Elaine Mitchell Attias
Matilde Attolico
Thomas Bendhem
Jasper Boersma
Keith & Helen Bolderson
Jeremy Bond
Brian Boylan
Mrs Elly Brook JP
Julian Brookstone
Paul & Ossi Burger
Debbi & Richard Burston
Yuen-Wei Chew
Martin Cliff
Carole & Neville Conrad
Conway Van Gelder
Coppard & Co.
Barry Cox
Curtis Brown Ltd
Peter Czernin
Deborah Davis
Chris & Jane Deering
Zöe Dominic
Robyn Durie

Lorraine Esdaile
Winston & Jean Fletcher
Nick Fraser
Jacqueline & Jonathan Gestetner
Michael Goddard
Carolyn Goldbart
Judy & Frank Grace
Byron Grote
Sue & Don Guiney
Hamilton Asper Management
Woodley Hapgood
Jan Harris
Phil Hobbs
Amanda Howard Associates
Mrs Martha Hummer-Bradley
Lisa Irwin-Burgess
Paul Kaju & Jane Peterson
Mr & Mrs T Kassem
Peter & Maria Kellner
Diana King
Clico Kingsbury
Lee & Thompson
Caroline & Robert Lee
Carole A Leng
Lady Lever
Colette & Peter Levy
Ann Lewis
Ian Mankin
Christopher Marcus
David Marks
Nicola McFarland
Mr & Mrs Roderick R McManigal
Mae Modiano
Eva Monley
Pat Morton
Georgia Oetker
Paul Oppenheimer
Janet & Michael Orr
Diana Parker
Maria Peacock
Pauline Pinder
Mr Thai Ping Wong
Jeremy Priestley
Simon Rebbechi
John & Rosemarie Reynolds
Samuel French Ltd
Bernice & Victor Sandelson
John Sandoe (Books) Ltd
Nicholas Selmes
Bernard Shapero
Jenny Sheridan
Lois Sieff OBE

Peregrine Simon
Brian D Smith
John Soderquist
The Spotlight
Max Stafford-Clark
Sue Stapely
June Summerill
Anthony Wigram
George & Moira Yip
Ms Tricia Young
Georgia Zaris

STAGE HANDS CIRCLE
Graham Billing
Andrew Cryer
Lindy Fletcher
Susan Hayden
Mr R Hopkins
Philip Hughes Trust
Dr A V Jones
Roger Jospe
Miss A Lind-Smith
Mr J Mills
Nevin Charitable Trust
Janet & Michael Orr
Jeremy Priestley
Ann Scurfield
Brian Smith
Harry Streets
Thai Ping Wong
Richard Wilson OBE
C C Wright

LONDON ARTS

THE ENGLISH STAGE COMPANY AT THE ROYAL COURT

The English Stage Company at the Royal Court opened in 1956 as a subsidised theatre producing new British plays, international plays and some classical revivals.

The first artistic director George Devine aimed to create a writers' theatre, 'a place where the dramatist is acknowledged as the fundamental creative force in the theatre and where the play is more important than the actors, the director, the designer'. The urgent need was to find a contemporary style in which the play, the acting, direction and design are all combined. He believed that 'the battle will be a long one to continue to create the right conditions for writers to work in'.

Devine aimed to discover 'hard-hitting, uncompromising writers whose plays are stimulating, provocative and exciting'. The Royal Court production of John Osborne's Look Back in Anger in May 1956 is now seen as the decisive starting point of modern British drama and the policy created a new generation of British playwrights. The first wave included John Osborne, Arnold Wesker, John Arden, Ann Jellicoe, N F Simpson and Edward Bond. Early seasons included new international plays by Bertolt Brecht, Eugène Ionesco, Samuel Beckett, Jean-Paul Sartre and Marguerite Duras.

The theatre started with the 400-seat proscenium Theatre Downstairs, and then in 1969 opened a second theatre, the 60-seat studio Theatre Upstairs. Some productions transfer to the West End, such as Caryl Churchill's Far Away, Conor McPherson's The Weir, Kevin Elyot's Mouth to Mouth and My Night With Reg. The Royal Court also co-produces plays which have transferred to the West End or toured internationally, such as Sebastian Barry's The Steward of Christendom and Mark Ravenhill's Shopping and Fucking (with Out of Joint), Martin McDonagh's The Beauty Queen Of Leenane (with Druid TC), Ayub Khan-Din's East is East (with Tamasha TC, and now a film).

Since 1994 the Royal Court's artistic policy has again been vigorously directed to finding and producing a new generation of playwrights. The writers include Joe Penhall, Rebecca Prichard, Michael Wynne, Nick Grosso, Judy Upton, Meredith Oakes, Sarah Kane, Anthony Neilson, Judith Johnson, James Stock, Jez Butterworth, Marina Carr, Simon Block, Martin McDonagh, Mark Ravenhill, Ayub Khan-Din, Tamantha Hammerschlag, Jess Walters, Che Walker, Conor McPherson, Simon Stephens, Richard Bean, Roy Williams, Gary Mitchell, Mick Mahoney, Rebecca Gilman, Christopher Shinn, Kia Corthron, David Gieselmann, Marius von Mayenburg, David Eldridge, Leo Butler, Zinnie Harris and Grae Cleugh. This expanded programme of new plays has been made possible through the support of A.S.K Theater Projects, the Jerwood Charitable Foundation, the American Friends of the Royal Court Theatre and many in association with the Royal National Theatre Studio.

The refurbished theatre in Sloane Square opened in February 2000, with a policy still inspired by the first artistic director George Devine. The Royal Court is an international theatre for new plays and new playwrights, and the work shapes contemporary drama in Britain and overseas.

ROYAL COURT THEATRE INTERNATIONAL DEPARTMENT

Since 1992 the Royal Court has placed a renewed emphasis on the development of international work and a creative dialogue now exists with innovative playwrights and practitioners in many different countries including Brazil, France, Germany, India, Palestine, Russia, Spain, Uganda and the United States. Many of these projects are supported by the British Council and the Genesis Foundation. The Royal Court's current international work includes: International Residency, an intensive four-week programme for emerging writers and directors from all parts of the world; International Exchange Programme which focuses on new writing from specific countries through partnerships with theatres in those countries; International Play Development, which offers an ongoing programme in countries developing a new play writing culture; and International Playwrights Season, a biennial event which offers full productions of plays in specially commissioned translations.

The Royal Court's exchange with Russian new writing began in 1999 since when the Royal Court has led a number of workshops in Moscow, Novosibirsk and Ykaterinburg. Vassily Sigarev took part in this play development work. Extracts from one of the projects developed in Russia - Moscow Open City - were performed as part of the International Playwrights Season 2000. In May 2001 the Royal Court presented a week of rehearsed readings New Plays from Russia. Plasticine is part of a wider focus on Russia in the International Playwrights Season 2002. The International Playwrights Season is produced by the Royal Court International Department:
Associate Director **Elyse Dodgson**
International Administrator **Natalie Highwood**
International Associate **Ramin Gray**
International Assistant **Rachel Toogood**

FOR THE ROYAL COURT

ARTISTIC

Artistic Director **Ian Rickson**
Assistant to the Artistic Director **Jo Luke**
Associate Director **Dominic Cooke**
Associate Director International **Elyse Dodgson**
Associate Director Casting **Lisa Makin**
Associate Directors* **Stephen Daldry, James Macdonald, Katie Mitchell, Max Stafford-Clark, Richard Wilson**
Literary Manager **Graham Whybrow**
Literary Associate **Stephen Jeffreys** *
Voice Associate **Patsy Rodenburg***
Casting Assistant **Amy Ball**
International Administrator **Natalie Highwood**
International Associate **Ramin Gray**
Resident Dramatist **Roy Williams**

YOUNG WRITERS' PROGRAMME

Associate Director **Ola Animashawun**
Education Officer **Christine Hope**
Outreach Worker **Lucy Dunkerley**
Writers Tutor **Simon Stephens***
Administrative Assistant **Lorna Rees**

PRODUCTION

Production Manager **Paul Handley**
Deputy Production Manager **Sue Bird**
Facilities Manager **Fran McElroy**
Production Assistant **Jane Ashfield**
Company Stage Manager **Cath Binks**
Head of Lighting **Johanna Town**
Lighting Deputy **Heidi Riley**
Assistant Electricians **Gavin Owen, Andrew Taylor**
Lighting Board Operator JTD **Richard Wright**
Head of Stage **Martin Riley**
Stage Deputy **Steven Stickler**
Stage Chargehand **Daniel Lockett**
Head of Sound **Paul Arditti**
Sound Deputy **Ian Dickinson**
Sound Operator JTD **Michael Winship** *
Head of Wardrobe **Iona Kenrick**
Wardrobe Deputy **Jackie Orton**

ENGLISH STAGE COMPANY

President
Jocelyn Herbert
Vice President
Joan Plowright CBE
Council
Chairwoman **Liz Calder**
Vice-Chairman **Anthony Burton**
Members
Martin Crimp
Judy Daish
Stephen Evans
Tamara Ingram
Phyllida Lloyd
James Midgley
Edward Miliband
Nicholas Wright
Alan Yentob

MANAGEMENT

Executive Director **Barbara Matthews**
Assistant to the Executive Director **Nia Janis**
General Manager **Diane Borger**
Administration Interns **Vanessa Cook, Juliette Goodman**
Finance Director **Sarah Preece**
Finance Officer **Rachel Harrison**
Finance Assistant **Martin Wheeler**
Accountant **Simone De Bruyker** *

MARKETING & PRESS

Head of Marketing **Penny Mills**
Head of Press **Ewan Thomson**
Marketing Officer **Charlotte Franklin**
Marketing and Press Assistant **Claire Christou**
Marketing Intern **Jennie Whitell**
Box Office Manager **Neil Grutchfield**
Deputy Box Office Manager **Valli Dakshinamurthi**
Duty Box Office Manager **Glen Bowman**
Box Office Sales Operators **Carol Pritchard, Steven Kuleshnyk**

DEVELOPMENT

Head of Development **Helen Salmon**
Development Associate **Susan Davenport** *
Sponsorship Manager **Rebecca Preston**
Development Officer **Alex Lawson**
Development Assistant **Chris James**
Development Intern **Vangel Efthimiadou**

FRONT OF HOUSE

Theatre Manager **Elizabeth Brown**
Deputy Theatre Manager **Jeremy Roberts**
Duty House Manager **Suzanne Kean, Paul McLaughlin, Neil Morris***
Bookshop Manager **Peggy Riley**
Assistant Bookshop Manager **Simon David**
Bookshop Assistants **Michael Chance, Jennie Fellows, Suzanne Kean,**
Stage Door/Reception **Hannah Caughlin, Simon David, Kelda Holmes, Hannah Lawrence, Tyrone Lucas, Andrew Pepper, Kathleen Smiley**
Thanks to all of our ushers

* part-time

Honorary Council
Sir Richard Eyre
Alan Grieve
Sir John Mortimer QC CBE

Advisory Council
Diana Bliss
Tina Brown
Allan Davis
Elyse Dodgson
Robert Fox
Jocelyn Herbert
Michael Hoffman
Hanif Kureishi
Jane Rayne
Ruth Rogers
James L. Tanner

A Nick Hern Book

Plasticine first published in Great Britain in 2002
as an original paperback by Nick Hern Books Limited,
14 Larden Road, London W3 7ST in association with
the Royal Court Theatre, London

Plasticine is published by arrangement with
Hartmann & Stauffacher, Cologne

Plasticine copyright © 2002 by Vassily Sigarev

Translation from the Russian copyright © 2002 by Sasha Dugdale

Vassily Sigarev and Sasha Dugdale have asserted their right
to be identified respectively as the author and the translator
of this work

Typeset by Country Setting, Kingsdown, Kent CT14 8ES
Printed in Great Britain by Bookmarque, Croydon, Surrey

A CIP catalogue record for this book is available from
the British Library

ISBN 185459 690 X

PLASTICINE

Vassily Sigarev

translated by Sasha Dugdale

It has passed
The roses are dead
Their petals float down
Why did I dream of roses
All the time
We hunted them together
We hunted out the roses . . .
. . . It has passed and the roses are forgotten.

Dino Campana

Characters

MAKSIM

LYOKHA (Alexei Vassiliev)

BRIDEGROOM (Slava)

BRIDE

SCHOOLTEACHER (Ludmila Ivanovna)

LYOKHA'S MOTHER

HEADMASTER (Oleg Petrovich)

MAKSIM'S GRANDMOTHER (Olga Ivanovna)

SPIRA

NEIGHBOUR

NATASHA

MAN IN T-SHIRT (Cadet)

BARE-CHESTED MAN (Sedoy)

SHE, HER (Tanya)

Various MEN, WOMEN and CHILDREN

1

*He sits on the floor in a room which is bare, apart from a
table, a bed and a carpet hanging on the wall. His fingers are
working plasticine into a strange shape. He finishes and puts
the strange thing he has created in a bowl of glutinous dirty-
white mixture. Then he takes the lead plates out of a car
battery and bangs them on the edge of the bed to knock the
residue off them, breaks them into pieces and puts them in
a pan. He fetches a small hob with a bare element, places
the pan on the hob and turns the hob on. He takes the bowl
and touches its contents with his hand: it is as hard as stone.
He scrapes out the plasticine. He looks into the pan – a small
lead-coloured pool of liquid reflects his face and a white pin
of light from the lampshade on the ceiling. He takes the pan
and pours the lead into the bowl. The remains of the plasticine
hiss, catching light, and flare up. Smoke rises to the ceiling
and goes in his eyes. The tears well up. He turns away, but
the tears continue to roll down his nose and then down to the
corners of his mouth. Now he is actually crying. He is sobbing.*

Crying as if he knew something . . .

The bowl cracks . . .

2

The entrance hall of a shabby five-storey block of flats.
MAKSIM *climbs up the stairs to the fourth floor. People pass
him on the way up. They are silent, their faces empty. The
stairway comes to an end. There is a door in front of*
MAKSIM. *It is open; a felt boot stuffed in the crack keeps
it ajar. There is a mirror hanging inside opposite the door.
A red plush tablecloth with a fringe hangs over it, covering it.*
MAKSIM *stops by the mirror and looks at it. The tablecloth
suddenly falls to the floor and* MAKSIM *sees his own reflection
in the mirror. He looks at it in amazement as if he was looking
at it for the first time.*

Someone touches him on the shoulder. MAKSIM *turns around
and sees a* WOMAN *in a black shawl.*

WOMAN. What you do that for? You shouldn't have. Are you a schoolmate of his?

MAKSIM *nods.*

Go on through . . .

MAKSIM *goes into the main room. It is full of people. In the middle of the room there is a coffin with its lid on.* MAKSIM *stands behind* TWO OLD WOMEN. *He stands on tiptoe, trying to look at the coffin.*

FIRST OLD WOMAN. Hey – don't push!

MAKSIM. You what?

FIRST OLD WOMAN. Get out of it.

MAKSIM *looks at her in bewilderment.*

I said get out of it.

MAKSIM. But I . . .

SECOND OLD WOMAN. Go on then.

MAKSIM *moves away.*

FIRST OLD WOMAN. There was one like him on the bus. He got right behind me and started to rub himself up and down on me. Got a hard-on straight away. I took a-hold of him and pulled his hair. The things that blimmin' go on. I mean, you'd think he was only a kid – but he was already getting it up . . .

A VOICE FROM THE ENTRANCE HALL. The crane is here.

The WOMAN *in the black shawl goes over to the window and looks out. A* LITTLE MAN *in an over-large jacket goes up to her.*

MAN. Where do you want the logs?

WOMAN. What? Oh . . . (*She was caught up in her own thoughts.*) Put them over there and here. It's all the same, isn't it . . .

The MAN *goes out and the* WOMAN *begins to open up the french windows onto the balcony. The windows are sealed for the winter and the doorframe is stuffed with rags. She rips the rags out, getting angry.*

WOMAN (*it isn't clear whom she is talking to*). Couldn't they have opened them up before now? The bastards . . .

She tugs at the balcony door and it flies open with a crash.
Cotton wool scatters from the doorframe.

VOICE. It won't go through there. It'll have to go through the
window.

WOMAN. You're a lot of help. Why am I killing myself . . .
You do it yourselves then – I've had about all I can take.

She goes out. A man stands on the window frame
and opens up the windows. People begin to leave the flat
together, as if by agreement. MAKSIM *leaves with everyone*
else. The SECOND OLD WOMAN *catches up with him;*
she stops and whispers something in his ear. MAKSIM
pales and runs off down the stairs. The SECOND OLD
WOMAN *smiles strangely.*

3

On the street outside. A lorry with a crane stands under the
window of the flat, surrounded by a crowd of people. Everyone
is looking up, watching the coffin being fixed to the jib of the
crane. MAKSIM *stands next to a* LAD *and a* GIRL.

GIRL. What's that for?

LAD. The hallway is too narrow for the coffin. It won't fit
through. My Nan had a flat like that. They unloaded her
though, and just carried her out. She was fat, so they had
a right lot of trouble.

GIRL. Oooh.

LAD. What if it fell, hey?

GIRL. What?

LAD. Land on his head, wouldn't he?

GIRL. C'mon, let's go.

LAD. He won't fall, will he? It's a company does it. Their stuff
is all tested.

VOICE FROM ABOVE. Take it away!

The jib of the crane begins to lower, swaying, like a tall
slender tree. A funeral march pipes up, although from where
it is not clear. MAKSIM *looks around for the source of the*
music. He sees the LITTLE MAN *in his over-large jacket*

with a tape-recorder hanging around his neck on a shoulder strap. The MAN *is stroking the black plastic body of the tape-recorder lovingly as if it were his only child.*

GIRL. So who are they burying then?

LAD. Some nut, I reckon. Hanged himself over a bird. Or so I've heard.

GIRL. What, really?

LAD. Like I said. I don't know. (*To* MAKSIM.) Hey, mate, any idea who they're burying?

MAKSIM. Spira.

LAD. Who?

MAKSIM. This . . . boy.

LAD. What sort of a boy? Who was he, then?

MAKSIM. Just a boy.

LAD. So what happened to him?

MAKSIM. He died.

LAD. I get it. You don't know fuck all, neither. (*He turns away.*)

By now the coffin has been lowered, taken off the jib and carried to a car with a stainless steel plaque on it. On the plaque there is a photograph of a little boy smiling. The crowd move after the coffin. Two WOMEN *in black dresses are left. One is an old woman, the other is younger, but they look almost identical. They are both drunk.*

MAKSIM *stops and looks at them.*

FIRST. Don't I even get the bloody clothes?

SECOND. What, to sell for booze? Not likely! I still have grandsons, you know. They'll get them.

FIRST. Oh right. So I don't exist anymore, eh?

SECOND. That's right!

FIRST. I was his Mother, you know!

SECOND. You're no Mother – you're just a slut! They should cut the wombs out of Mothers like you an' all.

FIRST. You're not giving us nothing, then?

SECOND. I should think not. Come on, get out of here. Don't make a scene. It's disgraceful.

FIRST. I'm still going to the cemetery.

SECOND. Oh you are, are you? You think you're going to the wake an' all?

FIRST. And the wake. It's my right.

SECOND. For the free booze?

FIRST. No. To mourn.

SECOND. Off you go then. Mourn! (*She walks away.*)

FIRST (*catches her up*). So you really not going to give me his stuff, then?

SECOND. No, I'm not.

FIRST. Oh you're not, eh?

SECOND. Get out of it, you useless tart!

FIRST. I'll sue you! (*Suddenly shouting.*) You sent him to his grave, you fucking witch! It was you! I knew it! You old bitch! You fucking evil witch! You sent my only child to his grave! It was you! (*She falls down crying.*)

The SECOND WOMAN *walks away quickly.*

FIRST (*to* MAKSIM). Come over here, eh?

MAKSIM. Fuck you, you slut! (*Walks off quickly in the opposite direction.*)

FIRST. What? Oh go on, give us a hand up . . .

MAKSIM. Piss off and die!

FIRST. Y'what? I know you, you little shit! I'll be round yours! Your Mum and Dad'll . . .

MAKSIM. Suck – my – cock!

He runs off. The WOMAN *shouts something after him. The funeral march starts up again, but suddenly slows down and finally cuts out altogether. The* LITTLE MAN *in his over-large jacket takes the cassette out of the tape-recorder. The tape has unravelled and caught on the head of the recorder and the* MAN *attempts to free the tape without success. He rips the tape out of the recorder, stuffs it into his pocket and runs over to the bus. The* FIRST WOMAN *runs towards the bus, too, but the doors of the bus close right in her face and it drives off. She shouts after it for a while, then she spits on the ground and swears.*

*Finally she quietens down and walks off down the road in
the same direction that the bus took. A* BARE-CHESTED
MAN *hangs over a first-floor balcony of the next block along.*

MAN. Not having a good day, eh?

WOMAN. Shut your mouth!

MAN. Come on. Fancy a drink?

WOMAN. Have you got one, then?

MAN. Yeah.

WOMAN. Alright.

MAN. Flat number ten. (*He disappears.*)

The WOMAN *gets a broken piece of mirror out of her
pocket and makes an attempt to pretty herself up. Then she
goes in the door of the block, smiling and contented.*

MAKSIM *has been watching all this and he turns and
walks down the road. Suddenly he sees* HER. SHE *is
walking towards him, carefully avoiding the puddles on the
pavement.* SHE *doesn't walk, she floats – all light, ethereal
and otherworldly.* MAKSIM *freezes as if under a spell.
He watches her. She turns the corner and disappears.*

4

In the men's toilets at school. MAKSIM *and* LYOKHA *are
smoking, hiding behind a partition wall. The cisterns are
hissing loudly.* LYOKHA *blows a smoke ring up to the ceiling
and smiles.*

MAKSIM. Didn't you go and see Spira off?

LYOKHA. Bet I didn't miss much.

MAKSIM. They didn't open the coffin.

LYOKHA. Reckon he was already rotting.

MAKSIM. Did you know her?

LYOKHA. Nice bit of totty. I wouldn't turn my nose up at her.
(*Throws the cigarette away.*) Finish your fag or you-know-
who will be sticking her nose in here again.

MAKSIM. Let her.

LYOKHA. Doesn't mean bugger all to you, does it? My Mum'll kill me though.

The door opens. MAKSIM *drops the cigarette into the toilet bowl.* LUDMILA IVANOVNA, *the Russian teacher, comes in. She is wearing a long drab brown dress.*

LUDMILA. Aha. I have you now. (*She comes over.*) Who have we got here?

MAKSIM *and* LYOKHA *turn to face the toilets and pretend to piss.*

Turn around then.

LYOKHA. In a sec.

LUDMILA. Come on, quickly.

LYOKHA. Just a sec.

LUDMILA. I said quickly!

LYOKHA *turns around, doing up his flies.*

Now you.

MAKSIM. I haven't finished.

LUDMILA. What haven't you finished?!

MAKSIM. Pissing.

LUDMILA. What did I hear you say? You say that again . . . (*Turns him around by force.*)

MAKSIM. Get your hands off me!

LUDMILA (*she is stunned for a second. Then she grabs* MAKSIM *by the hair and shakes him*). You little wretch! Are you raising your voice to me?

MAKSIM. Get you hands off!

LUDMILA. You . . . right. So that's how you want it . . .

MAKSIM. Take your hands off me, you cow!

LUDMILA. What?!

MAKSIM. Hands off! (*He wrenches himself free and walks to the door.*)

LUDMILA. Stop right there!

MAKSIM (*quietly*). Go fuck yourself.

LUDMILA. I told you to stop!

MAKSIM. You've got no right to come into the men's toilets . . .

LUDMILA. What did you say? Stop there!

MAKSIM *goes out.*

I don't know why you go around with that waster. His number was up a long time ago. But you – what are you doing? Can't you find yourself a nice normal friend? What are you doing with him?

LYOKHA. I'm not his friend . . .

LUDMILA. Oh, don't start.

LYOKHA. I'm not his friend.'

LUDMILA. He'll be thrown out before too long. Do you want to be thrown out with him?

LYOKHA. No.

LUDMILA. If I catch you with him again we'll be thinking about you as well. Do I make myself clear?

LYOKHA. Yes

LUDMILA. Move it.

LYOKHA *goes.*

(*Looking into the toilet bowl and sniffing.*) I've got you, you little viper. We're going to have a good talk.

5

MAKSIM *and* LYOKHA *are sitting in the playground.* LYOKHA *is eating an ice-cream cone.* MAKSIM *sits with his head lowered and is spitting on the ground. There is a large pool of saliva under his legs.*

LYOKHA. She says you're finished – they're going to chuck you out, Maxie.

MAKSIM. Like I mind.

LYOKHA. Really.

MAKSIM. So what?

LYOKHA. Don't you get it . . .

MAKSIM. . . . . Why has that cunt got it in for me? What have I ever done to her?

LYOKHA. Don't you get it? It's all 'cause of that . . . what's his name? Y'know, you punched his head in, in the changing rooms . . .

MAKSIM. So? The arsehole was going through everyone's pockets. They'd have thought it was me.

LYOKHA. Well he was her nephew or something.

MAKSIM. So? I know who he was.

LYOKHA. Well that's it.

MAKSIM. Well, she can . . . She comes into the bog again I'll give her something to look at . . .

LYOKHA. Are you going to piss on her or something?

MAKSIM. Like I give a shit about the old cow . . . I'll make a plasticine cock that comes down to my knees and she can get off on that.

LYOKHA (*laughing*). You're having me on!

MAKSIM. I'm not joking. You'll see.

LYOKHA. What? Right to your knees?

MAKSIM. We'll see.

LYOKHA. I can see it now. Want some ice-cream?

MAKSIM (*looks at the ice-cream*). No.

LYOKHA. Come to the cinema tonight. Guess what's on? Remember Bogatka was going on about watching Caligula on video. Porno movie.

MAKSIM. And?

LYOKHA. It's on at the cinema.

MAKSIM. They'll have cut out all the good bits.

LYOKHA. No way! My Mum and Dad went. Springs on their bed were squeaking all night. Means they didn't cut out the good bits.

MAKSIM. Let's go then.

LYOKHA (*looks at his watch*). Meet you at sevenish then. I'm fucking starving. We've got meatballs for tea. See you!

MAKSIM. See you.

LYOKHA *runs off.* MAKSIM *looks down into the pool of saliva. A drop of blood drips from his nose. He touches his*

*nose with his hand and it comes away bloody. He looks up
into the sky, craning his neck. Swifts are circling in the sky
like black dots. They fuss and rush through the air, filled
with some horror that only birds are prey to.* MAKSIM
closes his eyes.

6

It is evening. MAKSIM *and* LYOKHA *approach the back of
the cinema. They stop and look around.*

LYOKHA. Give it a whack, so it opens straight off.

They creep over to the cinema's exit door. MAKSIM,
*without saying a word, breaks into a run and hits the door
with his shoulder. Something falls with a bang and there is
a clanking sound.*

Have you done it?

MAKSIM. Hasn't budged.

LYOKHA. Try again. I'll stand guard.

MAKSIM *hits the door again. There is a bang and the
sound of a metal padlock coming loose and falling off.*
MAKSIM *bends double and clutches at his head.*

What's wrong, Maxie?

MAKSIM. My fucking head again . . .

LYOKHA. Did you get it open then?

MAKSIM. Reckon so.

LYOKHA. Let's go off and have a quick fag then.

MAKSIM. Let's go in.

LYOKHA. What, like – straight away?

MAKSIM. No point in wasting time.

LYOKHA. What if they heard us?

MAKSIM. Fuck them. (*He pulls at the door and it opens. The
sound of music by Prokofiev pours out through the door.*) In
you go.

LYOKHA. Alright. Shhh!

They enter and shut the door.

Darkness.

MAKSIM'S VOICE. Sit down on the floor.

LYOKHA'S VOICE. They're having a screw, can't you hear?
Open it up quickly.

MAKSIM'S VOICE. Wait a minute.

LYOKHA'S VOICE. Quickly, Maxie. We've missed loads
anyway.

*The inner door opens slightly and they can see a screen
with two naked women caressing each other on it.*

Phwoar! Get a look at that!

MAKSIM'S VOICE (*his voice is shaking*). Shhh!

LYOKHA'S VOICE. Shit! (*There is a long pause.*) Maxie.

MAKSIM *doesn't answer.*

Maxie . . .

MAKSIM'S VOICE. What?

LYOKHA'S VOICE. Maxie . . .

The sound of clothes rustling and unzipping.

MAKSIM'S VOICE. What you doing?

LYOKHA'S VOICE. Come on, Maxie. Don't be like that . . .

MAKSIM'S VOICE. Watch it . . .

LYOKHA'S VOICE. Just once, Maxie . . .

MAKSIM'S VOICE. Later . . .

LYOKHA'S VOICE. Just once, Max . . .

A scuffling noise, the sound of LYOKHA *breathing deeply.
He groans. On the screen two women urinate on the corpse
of a man who has just been murdered.*

7

In front of the cinema. MAKSIM *and* LYOKHA *stand in front
of a board with 'Caligula' painted on it in large red letters.*

MAKSIM. We could go for a cruise on Broadway.

LYOKHA. Pick someone up?

MAKSIM. We'll see.

LYOKHA. No. I'm going home. Mum'll do her nut. And I
could really eat something. I'll see you later.

MAKSIM. See you.

> LYOKHA *walks off.* MAKSIM *goes in the opposite
> direction. A black cat runs across the path in front of him. A
> woman, holding several bags and walking towards him,
> stops dead, as if rooted to the spot. She looks at* MAKSIM.
> *Only when* MAKSIM *has reached the point where the cat
> crossed does she start walking again.* MAKSIM *looks
> around and smiles. The woman also turns and smiles. The
> cat watches from the darkness with unblinking, burning eyes
> and without smiling.*

8

MAKSIM *walks past a café with blaring music and the
shouting of loud drunken voices coming from within. Inside he
can see tables laid with food and people dancing. By the
entrance a* BRIDEGROOM *in a bow-tie is sitting on a bin
with his bride on his lap. The* BRIDE *is smoking and talking
very loudly. Then she notices* MAKSIM *and throws her
cigarette away. She whispers something in the ear of the*
GROOM *and jumps down from his lap.*

BRIDE. Hey . . .

> MAKSIM *doesn't turn around.*

Hey, you!

> MAKSIM *stops and waits.*

(*Walking towards him, holding her skirt up and smiling.*)
Give us a fag, gorgeous!

MAKSIM. I've only got a packet of Prima.

BRIDE (*smiling*). Prima'll do lovely.

> MAKSIM *gets out the packet and gives her a cigarette. He
> puts a cigarette in his own mouth. He pulls out a lighter and
> holds it out to the* BRIDE.

Hang on. What's your name?

MAKSIM (*lights his own cigarette*). What's it to you?

BRIDE. Don't be like that.

MAKSIM. Alright. Max.

BRIDE. Maxie?

MAKSIM. Mm.

BRIDE. You know what, Maxie – take me away from here . . .

MAKSIM. Y'what?

BRIDE. Come on Maxie, let's get out of it, just you and me. I'll be your lover, Maxie. You should see my tits. (*She laughs.*) Go on, have a feel . . . (*She grabs* MAKSIM*'s hand and pulls it against her breasts.*) I want you, Maxie – I'm all wet between the legs for you, Maxie.

MAKSIM (*pulls back his hand and walks away*). You can go to . . .

BRIDE (*laughs*). You asked for it! (*Shouts to the* GROOM.) Slava, the pervert grabbed my tits! Stop there, you sneaky git!

The GROOM *jumps up and runs towards* MAKSIM.

You stay there, you bastard!

MAKSIM *keeps walking, without turning around.*

GROOM. Stop, you prick!

MAKSIM *stops.*

(*Runs up to him.*) What are we going to do with you, you little fucker? (*He lifts his hand threateningly.*)

MAKSIM *trembles.*

BRIDE. Rough him up, Slava! Aren't you fucking man enough?! Do him over! The bastard!

The GROOM *wavers for a few seconds and then punches* MAKSIM *in the face.* MAKSIM*'s cigarette flies in a different direction to his body.*

Finish him, Slav! Kick the pervert bastard's arse!

The GROOM *kicks* MAKSIM.

BRIDE (*brays with laughter, takes off her shoe and starts to hit* MAKSIM *with it*). Beat him senseless! Not man enough? Do him over!

GROOM. Alright. That's enough! (*He pulls away the bride.*)

The BRIDE *bends over and spits on* MAKSIM*'s head. They roar with laughter and run away.* MAKSIM *lies there some time without moving. Then he sits up, holding his head. His breath rattles. A car drives past and someone throws an empty beer bottle out of the car window. It lands next to* MAKSIM *but doesn't break. He stands up and walks back the way he came. Then he goes back, picks up the bottle and walks over to the café window. Right by the window the* BRIDE *is hugging a* WOMAN. *The* WOMAN *kisses her and is saying something animatedly. The* BRIDE *laughs. She is radiant.*

MAKSIM *knocks against the window with the bottle. The* BRIDE *stops the* WOMAN *with a gesture and presses against the window to look out.*

MAKSIM (*lifts the bottle threateningly*). Die, bitch!

The BRIDE *doesn't react. She probably doesn't even see him.* MAKSIM *doesn't move. There is a long pause and then the* BRIDE *turns back to the* WOMAN, *shrugging her shoulders.*

Fuck off, the lot of you!

He runs off, throwing the bottle through a flat window on his way. There is the sound of breaking glass.

9

MAKSIM *is walking towards the entrance hall of his block of flats. He stubs his cigarette out on the doorframe.*

VOICE BEHIND HIS BACK. Max . . .

MAKSIM *turns around. A boy is standing in the gate of the children's playground.*

BOY. Let's go.

He moves back. The light falls on his face and it becomes clear that he is the BOY *whose face was pictured on the stainless steel plaque.*

Let's go, Max.

MAKSIM *takes a few steps towards him, then stops.*

Come on. (*He moves away.*)

MAKSIM. Later, Spira . . .

BOY. Let's go . . .

MAKSIM. I'll be along . . .

He turns and runs into the entrance hall. The BOY *vanishes into the darkness.*

10

It is night time and dark in Maxim's room. MAKSIM *is lying in bed and holding his head. He stares at the ceiling. Suddenly he starts to whisper.*

MAKSIM. Don't . . . don't . . . it hurts . . . it hurts, Jesus, it hurts. Don't . . . don't . . . I can't take any more. Jesus, please. Please. Don't . . . (*He whimpers and clenches his teeth.*) Fucking stop it! I said stop! Stop!!! (*He bangs his head with the palm of his hand.*)

Silence. MAKSIM *climbs out of bed and turns on the light. He gets a box out from under the bed. There is a large ball of plasticine in the box.* MAKSIM *sits on the ground and starts shaping it. He has light blue bruises on his back from the bride's white shoes.*

11

The school toilets. MAKSIM *is smoking.* LYOKHA *is crouching next to him.*

LYOKHA. Hey, so guess what . . . I didn't go home last night, right. I was walking along and I saw this well fit babe purring towards me. Pissed as a . . . I go up to her all smooth, like, you know, and go 'fancy a beer, darling?' and she's fucking all over me. I get the beers and the Marlboro. We did some stuff on the stairs, I can tell you. Anyway, she's not from around here. And a bit of a headcase (*He puts his finger to his temple to illustrate.*).

MAKSIM. So what happened?

LYOKHA. What happened . . . I gave her one. She's all coy at first . . . All 'it's my first time' and all that crap. Then she puts the johnny on me herself. It was a right crush on the

stairs, I can tell you. It's the third time I've done it there.
You should have come with me. Her Aunt lives in that
tower-block the size of the Wall of China . . . She can . . .
Hey, who beat you up?

MAKSIM. It's nothing. Forget it.

LYOKHA. We could get them. I'll get some mates along. Who
were they?

MAKSIM. I don't know.

LYOKHA. Be like that then.

MAKSIM. It's nothing. Forget it.

The door opens.

LYOKHA. Watch out! (*He stands up in front of the urinals.*)

MAKSIM *goes over to the toilets and gets something out
from underneath his jumper.* LUDMILA IVANOVNA
appears, wearing the same brown dress.

LUDMILA. So it's you two again, is it? I warned you,
Vassiliev, didn't I?

LYOKHA. I wasn't smoking. You can smell my breath if you
like.

LUDMILA. That won't be necessary.

LYOKHA. I wasn't smoking, I said.

LUDMILA. I really don't care.

LYOKHA. I get it . . . Going to the toilet is against the law
now, is it?

LUDMILA. You are getting yourself in deeper and deeper. And
you, my sunshine, are you just going to stand there?

MAKSIM. Any law against it?

LUDMILA. Yes.

MAKSIM. Who says?

LUDMILA. I say. Now turn around.

MAKSIM. I haven't finished.

LUDMILA. Do my ears deceive me?

She turns him around by force and then pales. LYOKHA
also pales. MAKSIM *smiles. He is holding a long
plasticine penis against his flies. It is shiny and very real
looking. There is silence.*

12

The Russian language and literature classroom. There are
portraits of great writers along the walls. LUDMILA
IVANOVNA *sits behind the teacher's desk and opposite her*
across the desk sits LYOKHA'S MOTHER, *a formidable*
looking woman with short hair.

LYOKHA'S MOTHER. He was such a lovely boy. Used to
spend all his time at home. As soon as he started mixing
with that . . . he was like another person. Don't be hard on
him, Ludmila Ivanovna. Do you know what he says? He
says he's scared of that Maksim. Apparently Maksim said
he would turn the others against him if he didn't . . . go
round with him. He says he hits him all the time.

LUDMILA. He's quite capable of it.

LYOKHA'S MOTHER. Lyokha's promised to confirm this . . .
your . . . incident at the board meeting.

LUDMILA. They'll throw him out anyway. Before you can say
the word . . .

LYOKHA'S MOTHER. Then, if it isn't a big deal, I'd like you
to leave Lyokha right out of this. I'm sure I can, you know,
sort you out a pass at the swimming pool. I'm in charge
there.

LUDMILA. Quite. I understand. No need to ruin the boy's life.
Not a bad lad. Never a bad word . . .

LYOKHA'S MOTHER. The other one you can throw to the
dogs as far as I'm concerned. Make life easier for everyone.
Turns up here with his hard luck stories . . . Only takes one
of them to get a hold and the rest live in terror.

LUDMILA. Well he's finished as far as I'm concerned.

LYOKHA'S MOTHER. And quite right, too.

LUDMILA. He'll probably wind up in a street brawl and
that'll be that. As I see it, one less evil in the world to worry
about.

LYOKHA'S MOTHER. Quite, quite . . .

LUDMILA. So can I rely on you to sort my nephew out a pass,
too? We'd be down at the pool together.

LYOKHA'S MOTHER. It would be a pleasure, Ludmila
Ivanovna. Do a good person a good turn, I say.

13

The HEADMASTER*'s office. The* HEADMASTER, *a man of about forty, wearing a three-piece suit, sits behind the desk.* LUDMILA IVANOVNA *sits on his right-hand side. Opposite them sits* MAKSIM'S GRANDMOTHER *and* MAKSIM *stands behind her.*

HEADMASTER. So you see, Olga Ivanovna . . . that is your name, isn't it, Olga Ivanovna?

GRANDMOTHER. Yes.

HEADMASTER. Well, Olga Ivanovna, do you understand that we are excluding your Grandson from this educational establishment?

GRANDMOTHER. But . . . how?

LUDMILA. It's simple.

HEADMASTER. Ludmila Ivanovna, please. Maksim, surely you told your Grandmother?

MAKSIM. What difference does it make? I told you to give me the papers and leave it at that.

HEADMASTER. What do you mean – give them to you? According to the law it is the parents or guardians . . .

MAKSIM. Fine. Give them to her then.

HEADMASTER. No, it is not fine! You see, Olga Ivanovna . . . do I have your name right, Olga Ivanovna?

MAKSIM. Yes.

LUDMILA. Speak when you're spoken to.

HEADMASTER. You see, Olga Ivanovna, we were forced to turn to the extreme measure of expulsion.

GRANDMOTHER. But . . . what for then?

LUDMILA. His glorious deeds . . .

GRANDMOTHER. But what for then?

MAKSIM. Smacked her pickpocket nephew's face.

LUDMILA. That's enough you little wretch! Oleg Petrovich, I am utterly astounded. This woman, whoever she is, has the nerve to sit here and defend the total delinquent she dragged up. Do you, whatever-your-name-is, not even understand the situation?

GRANDMOTHER. What's that?

LUDMILA. I can't take any more of this, I really can't, Oleg Petrovich! You, do you understand that you've brought up a delinquent?

GRANDMOTHER. Oh he's not a de, er, linquent. He's a good boy. Brings me bedpans and all such when I'm bedridden and takes them away again. Does lovely plasticine models, an' all.

HEADMASTER. Not the ones he should be making.

LUDMILA. So he's a good boy is he?

GRANDMOTHER. Oh yes.

LUDMILA. Then I give up, Oleg Petrovich. I have no idea how to communicate with this woman. When did you last set foot on school premises, dear?

GRANDMOTHER. Well it's my legs, see . . .

LUDMILA. What about them?

GRANDMOTHER. I barely made it here.

LUDMILA. If you've got something wrong with your legs then maybe you shouldn't have taken on the boy's welfare. I am astounded, Oleg Petrovich, that she was allowed to at all. What on earth were they thinking of? It's a huge responsibility, dear.

GRANDMOTHER. Where else could he have gone?

LUDMILA. Don't give me any of that. The state, thank heavens, provides all the right conditions. You people haven't yet worked it out, have you? You attempt your home-grown welfare and the results are like this – (*She points to* MAKSIM.) Look – the result: drug addicts, delinquents and the dregs of society.

GRANDMOTHER. Why, you . . .

LUDMILA. Don't you get familiar with me . . . two can play at that game . . .

HEADMASTER. Ludmila Ivanovna, please – a little restraint.

LUDMILA. What use is restraint with these people? He should have been put away long ago – and her to boot.

MAKSIM. Shut your mouth, you old cow!

LUDMILA. What?

MAKSIM. Shut it, you bitch!

HEADMASTER. Maksim, Maksim.

MAKSIM. Maksim what, fuck it?!

GRANDMOTHER. Maksim.

MAKSIM. Come on, Nan. Let's go. What's the point of staying around to listen to the cow. Or she can get out.

LUDMILA. Did you hear that? Now you see what you've brought up!

MAKSIM. Shut your mouth, you bitch! (*He grabs a vase from the table.*) Or I'll knock your brains out.

LUDMILA (*jumping up from her chair in terror and hiding behind the headmaster*). Get rid of him, Oleg Petrovich! He's a psychopath! Whatever next! We should call the police!

HEADMASTER. Maksim, calm down.

MAKSIM. I tell you where the lot of you can go. Come on, Nan.

The GRANDMOTHER *gets up.* MAKSIM *puts the vase back in its place.*

HEADMASTER. I haven't finished yet.

MAKSIM. I have.

They leave.

LUDMILA. What a nightmare! They should shoot them at birth! Or before birth! Who has kids like that, anyway?

HEADMASTER. Go back to your class, Ludmila Ivanovna.

LUDMILA. . . . What?

HEADMASTER. Go back to your class.

14

MAKSIM *and his* GRANDMOTHER *come out of the school.* LYOKHA *is standing by the gates with a group of boys.*

MAKSIM. You go on, Nan. I'll catch you up. (*He stops and shouts.*) Hey, Lyokha, Lyokh!

LYOKHA *doesn't react.*

MAKSIM *goes up to him.*

Lyokha, are you deaf or something?

All the boys look at MAKSIM *and smile nastily.*

A BIG BOY WITH FLUFF ON HIS CHIN. Hey. The queer's turned up.

MAKSIM. Who's queer? You want to get your facts straight, mate.

BOY. You're a queer.

MAKSIM. Had enough of life, have you?

BOY. Oh yeah. Had enough. You queer.

SECOND BOY IN A RED JACKET. Lyosha told us all about how you were up for it in the cinema . . .

MAKSIM. What are you on about? (*Throws himself at the boy.*)

The BIG BOY *tries to punch him in the face but misses and hits his forehead. He grabs his own hand and howls in pain.* MAKSIM *runs at the* BIG BOY *but someone grabs his collar and pulls him down onto his back.*

LYOKHA. Do him – the fucking gay-boy!

The BOYS *all start kicking* MAKSIM.

(*Jeering.*) Finish him! In the face! Kick his arse!

LUDMILA IVANOVNA *comes out of the school and watches, smiling.*

15

MAKSIM *is washing in a fountain. His face is swollen and bruises are already coming up. The buttons on his denim jacket have been ripped off.*

He hears voices behind him.

FIRST. Mum, we're going to be late.

SECOND. We've still got time.

FIRST. How long?

SECOND. I don't know, I haven't got a watch. Ask that boy over there.

A pause

FIRST (*close up*). Excuse me . . .

> MAKSIM *looks up from under his arm. A* GIRL *is walking towards him. But not just any girl:* SHE *is walking towards him.* MAKSIM *looks at his face in the water.*

SHE. Could you tell me the time?

> MAKSIM *takes to his heels and runs. He runs and runs and runs.*

16

It is night again. Once more it is dark and MAKSIM *is lying in bed. He is holding his head as before and whimpering with his teeth clenched. Suddenly he shudders, listening to something. He shudders again. He gets out of bed and goes over to the window. He jerks the blind back and looks down. The same* BOY *is standing by the gate to the children's playground. He is saying something – his lips are moving, but he can't be heard.*

MAKSIM. I'll be along later, Spira . . .

> *The* BOY's *lips are moving and he recedes into the children's playground.*

Not yet.

> *The* BOY *shakes his head and speaks. He recedes further.*

Later . . .

> *Darkness swallows the* BOY. MAKSIM *pulls the blind shut. He gets the box of plasticine out from under the bed and starts kneading it.*

17

MAKSIM *is going down the stairs. His* NEIGHBOUR, *a man in glasses, comes up towards him.* MAKSIM *tries to pass him, but the neighbour bars his way.*

NEIGHBOUR. Got a light?

> MAKSIM *gets out his lighter and stretches it out towards him.*

(*Takes the lighter.*) I've got you, you little bugger. You set light to my bleeding box?

MAKSIM. Y'what?

NEIGHBOUR. I said, you set light to my bleeding box?

MAKSIM. What box?

NEIGHBOUR. My fucking letterbox. I'll twist your ear. (*He takes* MAKSIM *by the ear and twists it, sticking his tongue out with the effort.*)

MAKSIM *doesn't defend himself.*

I'll punch your fucking face in next time. D'you hear?

MAKSIM. Now give back my lighter.

NEIGHBOUR. What do you want it for, you little . . . Go on, hop it.

MAKSIM. Give me back my lighter.

NEIGHBOUR. So you can go round setting light to letterboxes?

MAKSIM. I didn't set light to it.

NEIGHBOUR. Get out of it!

MAKSIM. Give back the lighter.

NEIGHBOUR. Got a problem, you little sod?

MAKSIM. My lighter . . .

NEIGHBOUR. I'll give you what-for! (*Grabs* MAKSIM *by the scruff of the neck and shoves him.*)

MAKSIM *runs down the stairs, barely able to keep upright.*

Breeding like bloody rabbits and then the kids run wild and ruin all our lives, too. (*He goes up the stairs.*)

MAKSIM *stands on the landing, listening with his neck craned. A door slams.* MAKSIM *goes downstairs and collects up some papers from the letterboxes and climbs back up the stairs. He gets to the door where the* NEIGHBOUR *went in and pushes the newspaper behind the door handle. He feels for a match in his pocket and strikes it against the floor. The match breaks.* MAKSIM *gets out another and strikes again. The match lights.* MAKSIM *gives it time to take and then lights the paper with it. He goes down the stairs.*

CHILD'S VOICE BEHIND THE DOOR. Dad, smoke . . .

MAKSIM *races back to the door, rips the newspaper out from behind the handle, throws it on the floor and stamps on it. The door opens and the* NEIGHBOUR *sticks his head out.*

NEIGHBOUR. So it's you, you little git!

MAKSIM *runs downstairs.*

I'll kill you, you bastard! Trying to burn us to the ground, you little shit! I'll see you behind bars!

MAKSIM *runs out of the block.*

18

It is evening. MAKSIM *is sitting in the stand of a small stadium. He is eating a hunk of bread, breaking the pieces off with his fingers. There is no-one around. Frogs are croaking their bawdy mating songs in the park faintly, as if from a long, long way off.* MAKSIM *is listening. He is deep in thought and stares in front of him, eating mechanically. Two indistinct figures appear below: a man and a woman. They approach and it becomes clear that it is not a man, but an eighteen-year-old* BOY. *The* WOMAN *looks around thirty and she's slightly drunk. The boy has an unsealed bottle of vodka in his hand. They walk over to the stand at the bottom. They don't notice* MAKSIM. *The* BOY *puts the bottle down on the bench and begins touching the woman.*

WOMAN. Not so fast, hey . . . Let's have a drink first.

BOY (*speaks with difficulty – he has a lump in his throat*). Later.

WOMAN. What's the rush.

BOY (*he is trembling*). I want you.

WOMAN. Give us a kiss.

The BOY *kisses her, groping her ineptly.*

Cold hands.

BOY. I want you.

WOMAN. Am I beautiful?

BOY. Beautiful . . .

WOMAN. Do you love me?

BOY. I love you . . .

WOMAN. I love you, too. What's your name?

BOY. Dima . . . Please . . .

WOMAN. Will you marry me?

BOY. I'll marry you. Please . . .

WOMAN. Well, go on then (*She bends over and lifts up her skirt.*)

The BOY *unbuttons his flies and positions himself behind her. He is trembling all over.*

Not in there . . . Your first time then, is it, darling? . . . Not in there! What you doing now? Have you finished?

The BOY *moves away, buttoning up his flies.*

That was fast. You never even put it in.

The BOY *picks up the bottle of vodka from the bench and walks off.*

Hey! Where are you off to?

BOY. Piss off, you slut.

WOMAN. Stop!

BOY. What do you want?

WOMAN. Give us the bottle, you impotent git.

BOY. What did you say? (*Advances on her.*)

WOMAN (*backing off*). No need to get nasty . . . I'm off now, I am. My Dad's in the police . . . hey, don't be like that . . .

The BOY *kicks her in the stomach. She totters back and falls over.*

BOY. You fat cunt! I see you round here again, I'll finish you! Slut! (*He goes.*)

The WOMAN *waits until he has disappeared from sight. Then she gets up and brushes herself down, grumbling to herself.*

WOMAN. Impotent sod. Came in me knickers . . . And he was only a young bloke. Tight with the drink, the miserable bastard (*She sees* MAKSIM.) Hey! Who's that?

MAKSIM *doesn't answer. The* WOMAN *climbs up the steps.* MAKSIM *gets out a cigarette and lights it.*

Hallo . . .

MAKSIM *nods.*

Give us a fag?

MAKSIM *gives her a cigarette and lights it. His hands are shaking. The* WOMAN *takes a drag and sits down next to him.*

Out for a walk?

MAKSIM. Mm

WOMAN. My dog ran away. I'm out looking for it.

MAKSIM. What sort of dog would that be?

WOMAN. Oh, you know . . . with a pedigree.

MAKSIM. Right.

WOMAN. Not seen it then?

MAKSIM. Uh-huh.

WOMAN. You cold sitting there?

MAKSIM. No.

WOMAN. Let me warm you up. (*She hugs him.*)

MAKSIM *doesn't resist.*

(*Stroking him.*) I'm beautiful, aren't I?

MAKSIM. I don't know.

WOMAN. Will you marry me? My Dad owns a factory. He'll give you a car as a present. A Mercedes. And a five bedroom flat. Marry me?

MAKSIM *doesn't answer*

You love me . . . (*She touches his flies.*) There. You love me and I love you, too. Do you know how I love you? (*She kisses his face and whispers.*) My lover . . . my one and only . . . Do you love me? Prove your love to me. Prove it.

MAKSIM. How?

WOMAN. Kiss me there . . .

MAKSIM. What?

WOMAN. Kiss me there.

MAKSIM. Where?

WOMAN. There. (*She pulls up her skirt.*)

MAKSIM. What for?

WOMAN. I want you to.

MAKSIM. Why?

WOMAN. Kiss it. (*She bends him over.*)

MAKSIM (*pulling away*). Leave it out!

WOMAN. Kiss me, bastard! (*She pushes his face in her torn knickers.*) Kiss me, bastard! Kiss me if you love me!

MAKSIM *vomits on her. The* WOMAN *pushes him away.* MAKSIM *staggers back, blood dripping from his nose.*

Why?

MAKSIM. It's just . . .

WOMAN. What was that for? You fool. That hurt. You fool.

MAKSIM *makes his way down the stand climbing from row to row.*

Fool . . . it hurt . . . fool. It hurt. Fool . . . it hurt . . .

MAKSIM *breaks into a run.*

Fool . . . (*She picks up a half-digested piece of bread and stuffs it in her mouth.*) Fool . . .

19

It is night. MAKSIM *is in bed, holding his head and quietly wailing to himself. He looks at the ceiling with glassy eyes. The walls begin to pulse and the room presses in on him. The ceiling comes down on him. Everything is alive and moving. Everything is breathing, whispering to him, living. Everything is moving and pulsing and laughing at him. The room gets smaller and smaller. Now it is no longer a room, but a little box, the walls covered in black material. It is no longer a room, it is a coffin.* MAKSIM *cries out . . .*

20

It is day. MAKSIM *is sitting at the table and modelling the figure of a girl out of plasticine. There is a ring at the door.* MAKSIM *goes to open it.*

GRANDMOTHER'S VOICE. Maksim, get the door.

MAKSIM. I've got it. (*He opens the door.*)

LYOKHA *stands on the doorstep. He is holding a plastic bag filled with beer bottles.*

LYOKHA. Give us a hand, Maksim, eh?

MAKSIM. What do you want?

LYOKHA. Well I picked up this babe . . . with a place of her own . . . You know, the works . . . She goes to me, 'bring a friend' . . . she's got some other girl there or something. So I went round to Bogatka's house and he wasn't there, so I tried Dlinny and he's at home painting something with his Mum. So he couldn't go. So . . . I'm up shit creek . . . Help us out, Maxie.

MAKSIM. What sort of a girl?

LYOKHA. Phwoar! Well fit. I've just spent all my money on beer. Her friend'll be a total babe an' all, I reckon. Help out will you, Maxie. Let's go.

MAKSIM. Come in.

LYOKHA (*enters*). Get a move on, Maxie. She's waiting downstairs.

MAKSIM. I'll just get dressed.

LYOKHA. Get a move on.

MAKSIM *goes into his bedroom and gets dressed.*

(*Standing in the doorway.*) I've been up to some unreal stuff without you around. Do you know Bulka?

MAKSIM. Mm.

LYOKHA. I gave her a good one. We went to some girl's dacha with Bogatka and . . . phwoar . . . what we got up to! I drunk so much I fucking pissed myself. Guess what I did down at my Mum's swimming pool?

MAKSIM. What?

LYOKHA. I made a hole in the wall of the women's shower room. Well, in the door. Now I can get an eyeful whenever. The bodies in there. Wow! Like, all different women. Some of them have got grey hair, y'know down there . . . (*He roars with laughter.*) And you know what's-his-name? The one you punched a while back? The nephew . . .

MAKSIM. Well?

LYOKHA. Well, he's copped it.

MAKSIM. What?

LYOKHA. Drowned, didn't he?

MAKSIM. How?

LYOKHA. How d'you think? Mum did them both a free pass and he couldn't swim to save his life. The End.

MAKSIM. Fuck me.

LYOKHA. Serves him right. Worthless git. I went in the showers with him once and he hasn't got a hair on his body. And a little kiddy dick. Although he's a big fucker to look at. I mean, think about it – he was already in the fifth form. Why didn't the prick cop it before now . . . Then you'd still be at school. Should have told my Mum to sort a pass out for them ages ago. And that old cow has joined the God squad. She's all butter wouldn't melt now . . . Stopped hanging around the bogs anyway. You ready then?

MAKSIM. Mm.

LYOKHA. Hit the road, man!

MAKSIM. Let's go.

They go out onto the landing. MAKSIM *closes the door and they go down the stairs.*

LYOKHA. Maxie . . . I wanted to say . . . y'know . . . don't be pissed off about all that . . . stuff. It was like this . . . I was telling them about Caligula. Like what those men were doing . . . Anyway Dlinny starts talking some crap about how we must have done it an' all. He's such a wanker. And then you come up and that's it – they're off. I tried to pull them off you . . .

MAKSIM. Forget it. It's OK.

LYOKHA. No I mean it, Max.

MAKSIM. It's history.

LYOKHA. Need a fag?

MAKSIM. I've got some.

LYOKHA (*gets out a packet*). There you go. Packet of Camel. (*He thrusts the packet at* MAKSIM.) Take them all. You'll be breaking open your local crap in front of the babes otherwise. My Mum's been topping us up with cash recently.

21

By the entrance to the flats LYOKHA *looks around and* MAKSIM *squats, waiting.*

LYOKHA. She was here. Has the slut taken off? I told you to get a fucking move on. That's done it. Stupid cow. What shall we do?

A GIRL *of about twenty comes out from around the corner and waves at* LYOKHA.

(*Smiles.*) There she is! Come on, Maxie!

They walk towards the GIRL.

What do you think of her?

MAKSIM. Alright.

LYOKHA. Oh right. Got to be a supermodel for you, eh?

MAKSIM. The beer'll improve her.

LYOKHA. (*laughing*). Out of order . . .

They reach the GIRL.

Where were you, Natasha?

NATASHA. One of my old boyfriends lives here . . .

LYOKHA. Aha.

MAKSIM. Who's that then?

NATASHA. You won't know him. They've left anyway.

LYOKHA. This is Max.

NATASHA. Right. Let's go.

She walks off. MAKSIM *and* LYOKHA *follow her.*

LYOKHA. Where are we off to?

NATASHA. You know the barracks?

LYOKHA. Mm.

NATASHA. There's a block there.

LYOKHA. And?

NATASHA. That's where we're going.

LYOKHA. Your friend's not some dog is she? She won't frighten Maksim off?

NATASHA. She's cool. (*Smiles strangely.*)   .

LYOKHA. Hear that? Hold the bag for me.

He hands MAKSIM *the bag and catches up with*
NATASHA. *He puts his hand around her waist.*

NATASHA. You mad or something?

LYOKHA. What?

NATASHA. What's this for then? Half the town knows me
round here. You'll have your chance later. (*She removes his
hand.*)

LYOKHA. But I'm your bloke, right?

NATASHA. Yeah, that's right. Get moving. (*She starts walking
faster.*)

22

MAKSIM, LYOKHA *and* NATASHA *walk towards the
entrance of a four-storey block of flats which rises above the
low wooden roofs of the barracks. The door hangs on one
hinge.*

NATASHA. Through here.

LYOKHA. Fuck, it stinks in there. (*He touches the door.*)
Concentration camp you got yourselves here.

NATASHA. Let's go, then.

*They go in through the door and climb up the stairs. On the
landing between the ground floor and the first floor they
pass a row of twisted, broken metal letterboxes.*

LYOKHA. Nice place.

NATASHA. So?

LYOKHA (*holds onto* MAKSIM's *arm and whispers*). She's
not really going for me, is she . . . Maybe she fancies you.
If her friend isn't too rough then you can take this one.

MAKSIM. Let's see.

NATASHA. What are you doing?

LYOKHA. Coming. Which floor are we going to?

NATASHA. Fourth floor.

They climb the stairs. On the fourth floor NATASHA *is waiting for them by a derelict old wooden door. She puts a key in the lock.*

LYOKHA. Where's your friend, then?

NATASHA. I locked her in.

LYOKHA. Oh, right. What's her name?

NATASHA. Ask her yourself.

LYOKHA. I get it.

NATASHA (*opening the door*). Come in.

MAKSIM *and* LYOKHA *enter and take off their shoes.* NATASHA *locks the door and puts the key in her jeans pocket.*

LYOKHA. Where's your friend then?

NATASHA. In the main room.

LYOKHA (*walks into the room*). Nice . . . (*He stops dead.*)

NATASHA (*nudging* MAKSIM). Come on then.

MAKSIM *goes into the main room. Two* MEN *of about thirty are sitting there. One is bare to the waist. His body is covered with tattoos. The second is wearing a t-shirt. He is also tattooed.*

NATASHA (*to* LYOKHA, *smiling*). Eyes popping out, are they? Go on then, ask.

LYOKHA (*in a different voice*). What?

NATASHA. What you wanted to ask.

LYOKHA. I didn't want to ask nothing.

BARE-CHESTED MAN. Have the courage of your convictions, my friend. Sit down on the sofa and we'll have a heart-to-heart.

LYOKHA *sits down on the sofa. He is shaking.*

NATASHA. Scared? Shitting yourself, eh? (*Takes the plastic bag of bottles from* MAKSIM.) You sit down, an' all.

MAKSIM *sits next to* LYOKHA.

(*Puts the bag on the table.*) To think he was so tough back there . . . Going, 'I'll give you one you won't forget' and groping my arse an' all. (*She laughs.*)

BARE-CHESTED MAN (*opening the bottle with his eye muscles*). You're a lad, aren't you, my little friend?

MAN IN T-SHIRT. Just beer, is there?

NATASHA. He even went and got them himself . . . (*She sits down on the* BARE-CHESTED MAN*'s knees and takes the open bottle. She drinks. To the man in the t-shirt.*) You not drinking then, cadet?

CADET. Gives me the shits.

NATASHA. Lovely turn of phrase.

CADET. Gets my meaning across though.

NATASHA. Get us some vodka will you?

CADET. Time enough.

BARE-CHESTED MAN. Got names, have they?

NATASHA. That one's called Lyokha or something. Don't remember that one's.

BARE-CHESTED MAN. Hey, mongrel, what's your name?

MAKSIM. What's it to you?

NATASHA. One's got a name and the other's a tease.

CADET. Full of himself, isn't he?

NATASHA. As long as he's not full of disease . . .

CADET. I love 'em like that.

NATASHA. You made your choice, then? (*She laughs.*)

BARE-CHESTED MAN. So what's your name then, scumbag?

MAKSIM. How about Maksim.

NATASHA. Come for a pee, Max-y! (*Laughs.*)

BARE-CHESTED MAN (*opening another bottle of beer*). So Maksim, fancy a game of cards?

MAKSIM. I don't know how to play.

BARE-CHESTED MAN. Let me teach you. How about it, Alexei? Game of Strip-Jack? (*He smiles.*)

LYOKHA *shrugs his shoulders automatically.*

What's that?

LYOKHA. What?

NATASHA. Learn to speak properly and stop fucking around like some retard.

LYOKHA. If you like.

NATASHA. He's on board. Let's go.

BARE-CHESTED MAN. What about you, Maksim?

MAKSIM. I don't want to.

BARE-CHESTED MAN. What's that in aid of? Don't you like my face?

MAKSIM *doesn't answer.*

BARE-CHESTED MAN. Eh?

MAKSIM. I just don't fancy it . . .

CADET. I didn't neither, but my Mum still went and had me. Bitch, eh?

BARE-CHESTED MAN. What have you got against it, Maksim?

MAKSIM. I just don't fancy it.

BARE-CHESTED MAN. But we've already told you – that's no reason.

Pause.

Go on then, Maksim – one game and you're off . . .

LYOKHA. Go on Maksim – what's wrong with you?

NATASHA. Max-y . . .

MAKSIM. What?

NATASHA. Come for a pee! (*Laughs.*)

BARE-CHESTED MAN. What about it, Maksim?

MAKSIM. Alright then.

NATASHA. He's on board.

BARE-CHESTED MAN. Get the cards out, Tash. The boys want a game.

NATASHA (*gets up*). Where are they?

BARE-CHESTED MAN. In the kitchen.

NATASHA (*goes over to the kitchen. On the way she bends over* LYOKHA *and tweaks his cheek*). So what was it you were going to do to me?

LYOKHA. I can't remember.

NATASHA. Touch my arse. Go on. (*She turns her back to him.*) I said you could and I keep my word.

LYOKHA *doesn't move.*

Forgotten how to? Or don't you find it attractive no more?

BARE-CHESTED MAN. You get your trousers down, Tash. You're just sticking your jeans in his face and he could touch up his own jeans, if he wanted.

NATASHA. He's getting worried.

BARE-CHESTED MAN. No, you get them down. You said you keep your word, didn't you? Or don't you?

NATASHA *bares her buttocks.*

Now touch her. Go on, my friend. Look at the fucking fine arse on her.

LYOKHA *touches her buttocks gingerly.*

CADET. Don't just stroke them, like some girl. Give her a fucking pinch.

LYOKHA. How?

CADET. Like she's a tart.

NATASHA. Watch yourself!

CADET. Give her a pinch!

LYOKHA. How?

CADET. Do I have to show you, an' all?

LYOKHA *pinches her.*

NATASHA. That's enough. It hurts!

BARE-CHESTED MAN. Now kiss her where you hurt her.

LYOKHA *kisses her.*

CADET. Bite her!

NATASHA. Don't you dare.

CADET. Bite her or fucking feel it!

LYOKHA *bites her.*

NATASHA (*jumps away from him, pulling up her jeans*). Bastard! Shit! (*She kicks* LYOKHA *on the leg.*) Fuckhead. (*She pulls her jeans down again.*) Can you see anything?

CADET. Cellulite.

NATASHA. You can just fuck off. I'm going to bite you an' all. (*She goes over to the* CADET *and grabs his cheek in her mouth and bites as hard as she can.*)

The CADET *doesn't react.*

(*Pushes him away.*) Get me? (*She rubs her teeth.*) That fucking hurt.

The CADET *smiles. He has white teeth marks in his cheek.*

BARE-CHESTED MAN. Now go and get the cards, Tash. We wouldn't want to bore the boys.

NATASHA goes out to the kitchen

Was that the first time you've pinched a woman then, Alexei?

LYOKHA nods

Was it nice, then?

LYOKHA shrugs his shoulders.

Eh?

LYOKHA nods.

Eh?

LYOKHA. Yes.

CADET. You still a virgin then?

LYOKHA. What?

CADET. Still a little boy?

LYOKHA nods.

And not a little girl?

LYOKHA. No

CADET. Sure?

LYOKHA. No.

CADET. You're not sure? Perhaps we should check?

LYOKHA. I'm not a little girl.

CADET. How come you're still a virgin? A big grown-up boy like you?

LYOKHA. I don't know.

CADET. What d'you mean? No luck with the ladies?

LYOKHA. S'pose.

CADET. And why's that?

LYOKHA. Don't know.

CADET. You not asking nicely?

LYOKHA. Don't know.

CADET. Try Natasha. If you ask nicely . . .

NATASHA (*coming back with the cards*). What is it this time?

CADET. Lyokha here wants to get his leg over.

NATASHA (*turns to* LYOKHA). You can fucking . . .

LYOKHA. No I don't!

CADET. There's an offer now. You want to make use of the popular demand, Natash.

NATASHA (*to* LYOKHA). Watch yourself, you moron – just who d'you think you're turning down?

BARE-CHESTED MAN. That's enough, now. We're getting to you, aren't we, my friend?

LYOKHA *nods.*

Sit down then, you two. Let the game begin.

MAKSIM *and* LYOKHA *sit at the table*

(*Shuffling the deck.*) What are we going to play for?

LYOKHA. I don't know.

CADET. For flicks round the ear?

LYOKHA. No.

CADET. What then?

LYOKHA. You'll make it hurt.

BARE-CHESTED MAN. Are we just playing, then?

LYOKHA. Alright.

NATASHA (*laughing*). He's on board, then.

BARE-CHESTED MAN (*deals*). Two sides: two against two.

NATASHA. 'Just playing' to lose. (*She laughs.*)

BARE-CHESTED MAN. There you go.

They all take their cards and look at them.

Who's got the lowest card?

MAKSIM. Me.

BARE-CHESTED MAN. Take it away.

They play. NATASHA *stands next to the table, smiling.*

He's taken the forfeit.

CADET. No luck, mate?

NATASHA. Max –y . . .

MAKSIM. What?

NATASHA. Come for a pee. (*She laughs.*)

They play. There is silence.

BARE-CHESTED MAN. There. In the bag. (*He balances two cards on* LYOKHA's *shoulders like epaulettes.*)

LYOKHA *smiles sourly. A pause.*

NATASHA. Nailed you, did they, snotface?

LYOKHA. And?

NATASHA. You want to watch who you play cards with. (*She collects the cards.*)

LYOKHA (*stands up*). Right. We're off then.

BARE-CHESTED MAN. Off where?

LYOKHA. But you said a game and then we could go.

CADET. What about your gambling debts. We should settle them now, shouldn't we?

LYOKHA. I thought we were just playing . . .

NATASHA. Don't you know what 'just playing' means?

LYOKHA. No.

BARE-CHESTED MAN. Let me shed a little light for you . . . Tash, are you going to watch?

NATASHA. Don't think so. Hand us a beer.

The BARE-CHESTED MAN *gets two bottles out of the plastic bag and opens them. He gives one to* NATASHA *and gulps the second one down himself.*

Go on then. Amuse yourselves.

She goes out to the kitchen and sits by the window on a stool. She picks idly at the paint on the windowsill and drinks beer.

VOICE OF THE BARE-CHESTED MAN. Get your trousers down then, Aleksei.

LYOKHA'S VOICE. Please . . .

VOICE OF THE BARE-CHESTED MAN. Trousers down.

LYOKHA'S VOICE. Please, don't . . . please! Jesus! Help!

There is a scuffle.

VOICE OF THE BARE-CHESTED MAN. Keep still, fuck it!

LYOKHA'S VOICE. Please, don't . . . please don't . . . Please . . . I'll get my Mum to give you money . . . She runs the swimming pool . . . Please . . . Don't! Help me! Christ!

NATASHA. Will you fucking shut him up!

VOICE OF THE BARE-CHESTED MAN. Piss off! And you . . . I told you to keep still! You have your go then, Cadet!

VOICE OF THE CADET. He's grabbed hold of the chair!

VOICE OF THE BARE-CHESTED MAN. Whack him!

MAKSIM'S VOICE. Hands off, bastard!

The sound of a blow and a body falling to the ground.

VOICE OF THE BARE-CHESTED MAN. Get your hands round his neck! And you . . . keep still I said! Keep fucking still!

LYOKHA'S VOICE. PLEASE!!! (*He is screaming and crying.*)

The bare-chested man groans and pants. NATASHA smiles.

CADET'S VOICE. Sedoy, this one's foaming at the mouth,

VOICE OF THE BARE-CHESTED MAN. Don't interrupt me.

CADET'S VOICE. What are we going to do?

NATASHA. Grow up!

VOICE OF THE CADET. You give me that one – you can have a try with him.

SEDOY'S VOICE. Had enough? Go on then, take him!

More scuffling.

LYOKHA'S VOICE (*hoarsely*). Please . . .

SEDOY'S VOICE. Nice and easy.

NATASHA *laughs hysterically and beats the windowsill with the palm of her hand.*

23

It is night. Rain is pouring down. MAKSIM *and* LYOKHA *are walking along a deserted street.* LYOKHA *is walking slightly ahead. They are silent.*

LYOKHA (*stops and turns around*). Stop following me.

MAKSIM. We should go to the cops.

LYOKHA. Never. Understand?

MAKSIM. They'd do them . . .

LYOKHA. I said, never! Understand?

MAKSIM. Okay, okay.

LYOKHA. Anyway, you can piss off, you prick! This is all because of you! (*He walks away.*)

MAKSIM *follows him.*

Stop following me, you bastard! I said stop it! (*He walks off.*)

MAKSIM *stays standing there.* LYOKHA *goes another few yards and then turns around.*

If you so much as fucking breathe a word of this to anyone, I'll kill you. You understand? My mates will finish you! You and your nan, an' all. Is that clear? Bastard! Bastard! (*He starts crying.*) It's all because of you . . . My Mum told me to steer clear of you . . . Fuck it . . . Jesus . . . you bastard! Fuck off! Fuck off, I said! Why are you standing there? Fuck off!!!

MAKSIM *walks off down the road.*

LYOKHA *stands there. He is shouting, almost screaming. But suddenly . . .*

Max! Shit. Max! Stop, Max! Maxie!

MAKSIM *starts running.*

LYOKHA. Maxie, please! Stop! (*He runs after him and falls.
    He lies there.*) Maxie! Max! Max! Max! Maaaaaax . . .

24

MAKSIM *goes into his room and turns on the light. He goes
over to the table and sits down and takes the plasticine figure
and kneads it frenziedly. He looks down at the shapeless ball of
plasticine he is holding and wants to throw it back in the box.
But instead he starts to model. The ball takes on features:
arms, legs, a head, hair, a face . . . MAKSIM looks at it and
smiles.*

*A drop of blood falls from his nose and lands on the figure's
forehead. MAKSIM wipes it away neatly. He stands up,
undresses and turns off the light.*

25

GRANDMOTHER'S VOICE. Maksim . . . Maksim . . .

MAKSIM *opens his eyes and shudders. It is morning and
the room is light.*

GRANDMOTHER. Maksim, go down to the elections and buy
    me some minced beef.

MAKSIM. Where?

GRANDMOTHER. The town hall. They're holding the
    elections there and giving meat away cheap. Will you go
    down?

MAKSIM. What, right away?

GRANDMOTHER. It would be better. It'll all be gone soon.

MAKSIM. Alright.

GRANDMOTHER. Are you going then?

MAKSIM. Yes.

GRANDMOTHER. Here's some money. (*She puts it on the
    table.*) The shopping bag is in the hall. Where were you
    yesterday?

MAKSIM. What?

GRANDMOTHER. Where were you, I asked?

MAKSIM. Oh that . . .

GRANDMOTHER. Nevermind. Go on with you then . . .
They'll be sold out otherwise.

MAKSIM. I'm going.

His GRANDMOTHER *goes out and* MAKSIM *gets up and
dresses. He sees the flattened plasticine figure in his bed.*

26

MAKSIM, *holding a cloth shopping bag, walks through a
large hall filled with stalls. The crowds are buzzing around the
stalls. Some people are buying things, others just looking.*
MAKSIM *goes up to the long queue in front of the meat stall.*

MAKSIM (*to* WOMAN *at the end of the queue*). Is this where
the minced beef is?

WOMAN. This is it, son. Get in the queue behind me.

MAKSIM *stands behind the* WOMAN.

Did your Mum send you out then?

MAKSIM. What? Oh.

WOMAN. Good for you! Helping out your Mum like that.
They've got good sausage here as well – very cheap. You
could get some of that, too.

MAKSIM. I've only got enough for the mince.

WOMAN. You get the mince then, love. That's good, an' all.
Would you like a biscuit?

MAKSIM. Who, me?

WOMAN (*takes a biscuit out of her bag*). There you are.

MAKSIM. What for?

WOMAN. What do you mean? To eat.

MAKSIM. Don't want it.

WOMAN. Take it, take it. (*She puts it in his hand and turns
away.*)

MAKSIM *holds the biscuit, not knowing quite what to do
with it. He puts it into his bag.*

FAMILIAR VOICE. Mum, come over here!

MAKSIM stiffens and turns around. SHE *is standing by a shoe stall. She is holding some white high-heeled sandals. A beautiful woman,* HER MOTHER, *goes across to* HER. MAKSIM *watches.*

SHE. Look at these beauties.

MOTHER. I can see them. (*She turns to leave.*)

SHE. Buy them, Mum.

MOTHER. Haven't you got enough sandals?

SHE. Not like these.

MOTHER. You've got others.

SHE. But, Mum . . .

MOTHER. No.

SHE. But, Mum . . .

MOTHER. I said no. (*She walks away.*)

SHE (*walks off behind her still holding the sandals*). But, Mum!

STALLHOLDER. Hey! Where you going with those!

MOTHER. Put them back, Tanya. (*She tries to take the shoes away.*)

TANYA. But, Mum . . .

MOTHER. Put them back! (*She grabs the shoes.*)

TANYA. Stupid cow! You'd have bought them for Galka but you don't want to buy them for me. Stupid cow! I hate you! I'm going to live with Dad! And you can go and live with your Galka! Two stupid cows together! (*She starts crying.*)

The MOTHER *puts the shoes back on the stall and drags* TANYA *away by the arm. Her face is distorted with crying.*

Don't touch me, you stupid cow! You're not my Mum anymore! Let go of me! Let go! Stupid, stupid cow! I wish you'd die!

STALLHOLDER. What a silly tart, eh.

MAKSIM *looks at the sandals. He is pale. A* WOMAN *comes up behind him with a bag which is bulging and straining at the seams.*

WOMAN WITH BAG. You in line?

MAKSIM. What?

WOMAN WITH BAG. Are you in line?

MAKSIM. No . . .

WOMAN WITH BAG. Out of the way then.

> MAKSIM *moves to one side, but then staggers and drops to the floor.*

WOMAN (*runs over to him and lifts his head.*) What's wrong, son? Are you sick? Sick, eh?

WOMAN WITH BAG. He's probably some druggie . . .

WOMAN. I've got to get him outside into the fresh air. Mind my bag, will you?

WOMAN WITH BAG. Anything else? Seen the size of mine?

OTHERS IN THE QUEUE. Go on – we'll watch it.

> *The* WOMAN *lifts* MAKSIM *and carries him out onto the street. She puts him down on a bench and fans him with her hand.* MAKSIM *opens his eyes and looks at her.*

WOMAN. Feeling a bit better?

> MAKSIM *nods.*

Not enough air. It was a bit stuffy in there. All those people. Now you've got your breath back you'll be feeling better.

> MAKSIM *gets up.*

You stay there and I'll buy you everything and then take you home.

MAKSIM. No. Don't do that.

WOMAN. What do you mean, don't do that? Got to help your Mum.

MAKSIM. I haven't got one.

WOMAN. What haven't you got?

MAKSIM (*grinning*). A Mum.

WOMAN. What do you mean? Where is she?

MAKSIM. Flown away. (*He walks off.*)

WOMAN (*following him*). Oh, what a shame . . . Hey, where are you going? You wanted some mince, didn't you . . .

MAKSIM. Leave me alone!

The WOMAN *is stunned.*

(*Shouting.*) Get off my back, I said! What d'you want?!
Your biscuit back? Take it! (*He gets it out of his bag and
throws it at the woman.*) You're all getting to me, you
bitches . . . You know where you can all go!

He runs off.

The WOMAN *watches him go. She looks utterly bewildered.*

27

MAKSIM *runs into the block and up the stairs. He goes past
his own door and up to the top floor. He climbs into the attic
space. Startled pigeons flock out of the way and take off, flying
down to the street.* MAKSIM *climbs through the window onto
the grey slate roof and goes to the edge. He looks down. People
are scurrying around like ants down there. Running about their
business and always running late; saying hallo and goodbye to
each other in the same breath; throwing cigarette butts at bins
and missing them; telling jokes and then laughing at them
themselves. Tripping on their left side and spitting over their
left shoulder, tripping on their right and smiling; blowing their
noses onto the ground and then treading on the phlegm
themselves, finding kopecks and losing roubles, running after
buses they can't catch, meeting and parting, feeling joy and
grief, love and hate. But none of them look up into the air. Up,
to where the pigeons are darting in the sky, the rain is born
and where* MAKSIM *is standing on the edge.*

MAKSIM (*closing his eyes*). Fuck the lot of you.

28

MAKSIM *goes into the flat holding a bag with something in it.
He goes towards his* GRANDMOTHER's *room and opens the
door and looks in.*

MAKSIM. Nan, where do you want the meat?

Silence

Nan . . .

No answer.

Nan . . . (*He goes into the room.*)

29

In MAKSIM*'s room.* MAKSIM *is sitting on the floor, modelling a knuckleduster out of plasticine. He has a plate of diluted alabaster in front of him. When he has finished modelling he presses the plasticine into the alabaster. He takes out the lead battery plates and knocks the residue off them on the edge of the bed. He goes out and comes back with a hob and a pan. He turns on the hob and puts the pan on it. He breaks the lead plates and puts the pieces in the pan. He takes the plate of alabaster and cleans the plasticine out of it. Then he pours the molten lead into the cast. Smoke pours from the plate and makes his eyes fill with tears.* MAKSIM *turns away. But then he starts to cry in earnest, sobbing violently, anguishedly. The plate snaps.*

30

MAKSIM *leaves the flat, closing the door quietly and locking it. Then he unlocks it again and leaves the key in the lock. He goes over to the neighbouring flat and rings on the door. He waits but no-one answers. He tries another flat. There is a pause.*

CHILD'S VOICE. Who's there?

MAKSIM. . . . Your neighbour.

VOICE. There's no-one home.

MAKSIM. My Nan . . . she's . . . tell someone, will you . . .

VOICE. There's no-one home.

MAKSIM. My Nan . . . she's . . . tell someone, alright?

VOICE. There's no-one home.

MAKSIM. Tell someone, will you . . .

He runs downstairs

VOICE. Mum says I'm not allowed to open the door . . .

31

MAKSIM *runs out of the block and bumps into the* NEIGHBOUR *with the burnt letterbox.*

NEIGHBOUR. Hey! Stop, you! I've got you now, you bastard!

MAKSIM. Just keep walking away . . .

NEIGHBOUR. What? Into the block with you. (*He goes up to* MAKSIM.)

MAKSIM. Just keep walking . . . (*He puts his hand in his pocket.*)

NEIGHBOUR. What? What have you got there?

MAKSIM. Just keep walking!

NEIGHBOUR (*retreating*). Eh! You got a knife?

MAKSIM (*going towards him*). I said, keep walking . . .

NEIGHBOUR. Help! Someone help! He's trying to kill me! Call the police! (*He runs off.*)

MAKSIM *runs in the other direction.*

32

MAKSIM *approaches the four-storey building amongst the wooden barracks. He goes through the door hanging on one hinge and climbs up the stairs, past the warped and broken letterboxes, to the fourth floor. He stands in front of that same derelict old door. He stands in front of it for a long time, holding his breath. Then he walks away and starts to go back down the stairs. He stops, as if remembering something. He climbs back up the stairs and puts his ear to the door and listens.*

He knocks . . .

The sound of footsteps on the other side. MAKSIM *stiffens and adopts a belligerent pose. He looks at his hand. The sound of bolts being drawn back . . .* MAKSIM *puts his hand into the pocket of his denim jacket and tries to pull out the knuckleduster. It won't come out. The door opens slightly and the* CADET's *head appears in the opening.* MAKSIM *lashes out with his bare hand and hits the doorframe. He punches again. The* CADET *moves his face away and pulls at the handle, trying to shut the door. The door hits* MAKSIM's *hand. The wood splits and bends. The lock breaks off and flies across the landing.* MAKSIM *drops to the ground as if felled.*

CADET'S VOICE. Sedoy, give us a hand!

SEDOY'S VOICE. What's going on?

CADET'S VOICE. Some fucker just tried to kill me!

SEDOY *runs out onto the landing in his pants. The* CADET *stands behind him holding the door handle in his hand.*

SEDOY. Did you knock him out?

CADET. Don't know.

SEDOY. Get him in the flat.

The CADET *grabs* MAKSIM *by the collar and drags him into the flat.*

33

Darkness

NATASHA'S VOICE. You gone out of your fucking mind?

SEDOY'S VOICE. Cadet broke his arm in the door.

NATASHA'S VOICE. Like I care. Get him out of here.

CADET'S VOICE. Alright.

NATASHA'S VOICE. Get him out!

SEDOY'S VOICE. What's your problem, you tart?

NATASHA'S VOICE. Fucking me off!

SEDOY'S VOICE. Who's fucking you off?

NATASHA'S VOICE. You are!

MAKSIM *opens his eyes.*

CADET. He's coming round.

SEDOY (*goes over and squats next to* MAKSIM). Hallo, my lovely.

NATASHA. Get rid of him, Sedoy.

CADET. Yeah, what are we going to do with him, Sedoy?

SEDOY. I'm thinking. (*To* MAKSIM.) What are we going to do with you then, my lovely?

MAKSIM *puts his left hand in his pocket.*

What have you got in there? (*He puts his hand in* MAKSIM*'s pocket and pulls out the knuckleduster.*) Oh I see . . . This was for me, right? (*He tries it on, but it doesn't fit his hand, so he just holds it in his fist and punches* MAKSIM *in the face with it.*)

NATASHA. What the fuck are you doing?

CADET. Stop that, Sedoy.

SEDOY. I'm finished now (*He punches* MAKSIM *once again.*)

NATASHA. What are you fucking doing? (*She pushes* SEDOY *away from* MAKSIM.)

SEDOY (*standing up*). What's wrong with you, you cunt? I'll fucking well finish you off while I'm about it.

CADET. Don't, Sedoy . . .

SEDOY. I've finished, haven't I? (*He kicks* MAKSIM *in the head.*)

NATASHA. You're fucking out of your mind. (*She goes into the kitchen.*)

SEDOY. Can't let him go like that, anyway. When they put the plaster on his arm they'll want to know what happened . . . and he'll squeal . . . Pick him up.

CADET. Where are we taking him?

SEDOY. The landing.

CADET. Why?

SEDOY. Pick him up!

They pick MAKSIM *up, carry him out onto the landing and go down one flight of stairs.*

Open the window.

CADET. Why?

SEDOY. Just do it!

MAKSIM. My Nan . . . she's . . .

SEDOY. Yeah, yeah . . . Get a fucking move on, cadet.

The CADET *opens the window.*

MAKSIM. I won't do it again.

SEDOY. You won't.

The window is open.

Lift him up.

They lift MAKSIM up and push him out of the window.

MAKSIM. Please . . .

SEDOY. Fuck it, cadet!

CADET. He's grabbed hold of my shirt!

SEDOY *beats* MAKSIM*'s hand. Again and again and again.*

He's pissed himself, Sedoy!

MAKSIM *looks down. By the entrance to the block* SHE *is standing, looking up with* HER *neck craned.* SHE *is wearing high-heeled white sandals and showing them off to* MAKSIM, *smiling and laughing noiselessly.* SHE *sticks out her tongue at him and then lifts her skirt and strokes her legs.* SHE *runs her hand between her legs and over her breasts.* SHE *wriggles in delight and laughs again. Then suddenly* SHE *turns and runs away.*

There is no one down there. It is deserted.

MAKSIM *closes his eyes.*

Darkness.